TO ALL MY GRANDCHILDREN

TO ALL MY GRANDCHILDREN

Lessons in Indonesian Cooking

LEONIE SAMUEL-HOOL

Illustrated by Alonso Gonzalez

LIPLOP PRESS   *BERKELEY*

1981

Printed in the United States of America.

Library of Congress Catalog Card Number 80-84766
ISBN 0-936016-50-7 (hardcover)
ISBN 0-936016-75-2 (paperback)

This book was edited and prepared for publication by William Hool, Sarah Satterlee, and Christopher Weills.
Book Design and Typography: Sarah Satterlee
Proofreading: Linda Morrison and Audrey Weills

Contents

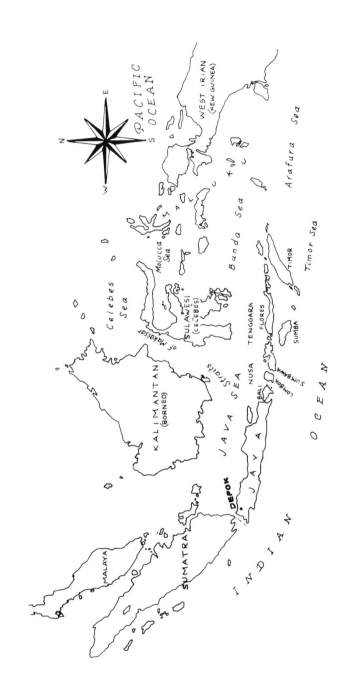

Indonesia

ABOUT THE AUTHOR

The life and background of the author are as unusual as this cookbook she has written. Marazionie Leonie Samuel was born of Javanese and Chinese parents on April 6, 1924, in Depok, Indonesia. Indonesia was then a Dutch colony called Netherland Indies, and Depok was a small Christian community on the island of Java, not far from the capital, Jakarta, then known as Batavia. Depok had been the landholding of a wealthy East Indies Company official named Cornelius Chastelein, who, upon his death in 1714, deeded the land and his cattle to the eleven slave families he had owned. They had already been given their freedom and Dutch citizenship, as well as the names Isakh, Joseph, Jonathans, Bacas, Laurens, Loen, Soedira, Tholense, Jordan, Jacob, and Samuel. The slaves, who had come from many islands of the Indonesian archipelago including Bali, Celebes, Sumatra, and the Moluccas, found themselves enormously wealthy.

Because the preparation of food has always been of extreme importance to all Indonesians, the Depokers' new-found wealth quite naturally resulted in the creation of a society in which everything, especially religious celebrations, centered around food. And as a consequence of the diverse ethnic backgrounds of the slaves, the varied cuisines of the different Indonesian islands were brought together as never before. The community's best cooks held the highest places of honor and respect, and famous cooks earned reputations that lasted for generations. Recipes were passed down within families in the same manner as jewels and property. Huge feasts were a common occurrence and often required as many as ten cooks and twenty helpers who prepared the food for several days in advance. In a country unequalled for its profusion of spices, vegetables, and fruit, Depok society, at its height, was probably unsurpassed in culinary variety and perfection.

Leonie Samuel, who seemed born with a love of cooking, achieved fame within Depok society while still a teenager. Her mother, father, and grandmother were all famous cooks—her father had five restaurants in the cities of Bandung and Bogor. Following in her father's footsteps, Leonie opened her first restaurant when she was just seventeen. And because Java was a Dutch colony, her father Indonesian, and her mother and grandmother Chinese, Leonie learned to cook the food of three cultures.

When she was twenty, Leonie Samuel moved to Holland where she lived for sixteen years while raising her five children. In 1960 she emigrated to the United States, and in 1969 opened The Rice Table restaurant in San Rafael, California, which has been called "the best Indonesian restaurant in the United States, and probably the world." She has told us that she will always resist expanding her restaurant so that she can continue to spice every dish herself.

MEASUREMENTS

Leonie only reluctantly agreed to write down measurements for quantities of salt. She wanted to say only, "Salt to taste." The ideal quantity depends on the individuality of the ingredients, the saltiness of a particular soy sauce, and your own taste.

Actually, Leonie was reluctant to note the quantities of spices for any dish. She says that, in Depok, whenever a recipe is given to an acquaintance, it is done orally and only the ingredients are told—except for one, which is kept for family members only. Each cook then spices to his or her own particular taste and fills in what is assumed missing. Leonie, however, has given the complete recipes for her taste, and the tastes of her family, expecting that everyone will experiment with his or her own variations.

Leonie has told us that her grandmother taught her that a good cook should know each particular diner's taste and try to please it. If there are diners who are strangers, they should be asked their particular tastes before the dinner is prepared, if at all possible.

Leonie is probably laughing about these recipes with her "exact" measurements. Use them as guidelines, but we hope you will cook to please your own taste, and those of the fortunate family and friends you serve.

SPICES

A section on Indonesian spices follows the recipes, on page 85, and should be referred to when desired. Below each recipe we have given the English translation, when there is one, of the spice used, and the page in the spice section where it is described.

Leonie had hoped to include a comprehensive list of available sources for Indonesian spices. However, as few retail outlets have complete lines of Indonesian spices and as she didn't want to recommend anything without personal knowledge, she will make the spices available through The Rice Table. Please write for a price list. And if you have any questions or comments, she would be happy to respond.

Leonie Hool
The Rice Table
1617 Fourth Street
San Rafael, California 94901

SERVINGS

An Indonesian meal is always made up of rice, at least one or two dishes to go with the rice, a *sambal*, or hot sauce, and usually a *sayur*, or dish with a watery sauce similar to a soup. The number of people eating and the importance of the occasion determine the number of dishes to be served. Leonie has given the approximate number of servings each recipe affords if only one or two side dishes are to be served with rice. Pickled vegetables and other condiments which can be stored have no suggested number of servings.

LEFTOVERS

As most Indonesians do not have refrigeration available, food is always intended to be eaten the day it is cooked. In cooler climates, and with the luxury of refrigerators, we feel that many cooked dishes, served as leftovers, benefit from standing overnight so that the spices and sauces more, completely penetrate the meat or fish. We know, however, that Leonie follows her grandmother's advice and, except in the hardest of times, cooks all her food fresh daily. She has told us, though, that she often enjoys food after it has cooled, especially chili pepper dishes, when eaten with warm rice.

GLOSSARY

A glossary of Indonesian words used in the text is included on page 101 for reference.

OUR APOLOGIES AND THANKS

We are only sorry that, in this book of Leonie's, we are unable to include that certain indescribable something that Leonie says all great cooks impart to their food by the "touch" of their hand. But we needn't worry—if you love to cook, you will add that very special ingredient, your own "touch."

We extend our sincerest thanks to all of Leonie's grandchildren who made this book possible. While we were enjoying one of many memorable dinners in her restaurant, Leonie told us that she was writing down some recipes and remembrances for her grandchildren. When she showed them to us, we found them such enjoyable reading that we convinced her to share them with others as well as her family. Here, then, is Leonie's gift to her grandchildren, and to you. *May your rice never burn!*

William Hool
Sarah Satterlee
Christopher Weills

Java

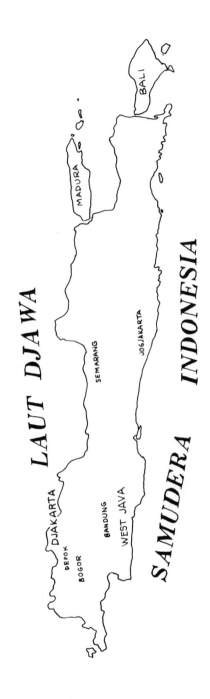

To All My Grandchildren

I was always taught that cookbooks, like spoons and cups used to measure cooking ingredients, were disgraceful things to have in a kitchen. Grandma only measured with her eyes and sometimes her hand, and she said that cooking could only be learned by watching another person and by learning "imagination in taste." Although I know that Grandma was almost always right about cooking, you, my grandchildren, cannot all be as close to me as I was to her because we live so far apart in America, and I don't know which, if any of you, may want to make cooking an important part of your life. So I have asked Grandma's forgiveness as well as the blessing of Dewi Sri, the Goddess of Rice, and will write down for you how I was taught to cook and a little about the cooks who taught me what they knew, as well as some of the recipes I have learned.

Your great-great-grandmother, who was my Grandma, took me as her apprentice even before I was nine. She loved cooking and it was as much a part of her religion as church would be to someone else. When I was very young, I wanted to cook more than I wanted toys or dolls, but before I was even allowed to touch uncooked food, I had to learn respect for the many spirits that lived in Grandma's kitchen. Some were imaginary, to teach respect to little girls—like the small spirits that lived on the shelves and always wanted to be clean. But there were other spirits who were very serious indeed. I think I should tell you about Dewi Sri so that you will understand a little about the spirits of Java and so understand the customs of the many aunts, uncles, and cousins whom you have never met.

THE LEGEND OF DEWI SRI

When I was very young, Grandma and Nanny told me the legend of Dewi Sri, who lived many thousands of years in the past, in the time of powerful wizards and great magic. Dewi Sri was a beautiful princess who had been born into the royal family of East Java and all its wealth which ordinary people couldn't even imagine. Well, Dewi Sri fell in love with a poor rice farmer from another island, but because he was not of royal blood, she was not permitted to marry him. Dewi Sri loved the poor farmer so much that she died of a broken heart. On the seventh day after her death, and while the people were still crying for the beautiful princess, a huge python snake was seen crawling from the grave of Dewi Sri and then out into the rice paddies. From that day on, Dewi Sri's spirit often visited farmers in the form of a snake and talked to them and blessed their crops. Any rice field she visited became more fruitful than it ever had been before and Dewi Sri became the most loved of all the Javanese goddesses. And that is why no farmer, to this day, will ever kill a large snake.

You can imagine why the spirit of Dewi Sri is so important to people who eat rice with every meal and why they love and respect her so. She always tries to bring forth bountiful crops and she represents the great abundance that God has always given the people of Java.

GRANDMA'S KITCHEN

Grandma was Chinese and loved food so much that she was always in the kitchen chopping, slicing, mixing, and tasting. I remember so well seeing her sitting in her rocking chair at the end of the long wooden kitchen table, laughing and chewing on betel nut, or smoking her black Java cigars, while she prepared the family food and ordered the servants about. She always had a leather whip at her side which she would crack in the air to get attention from the servants. They were never struck, though, and they loved and respected Grandma as did everyone who knew her.

Grandma was short and you would probably call her fat if you saw her. She weighed over two hundred pounds. Her face was pretty and her complexion was perfect, without a single wrinkle or blemish. Her hands and feet were dainty and her skin was almost white. Grandma was always happy and when she laughed the laughter rolled up and down her body in great waves. She looked very much like the fat and happy Buddha in her bedroom where she burned incense. She always wore a white lace *kebaya*, or blouse, and the most expensive, handpainted sarongs that could be bought. Her teeth were black-red from chewing betel nut, except for her two front teeth—which were missing. There were no real dentists in her day.

Grandma came to live with us when my Grandpa died, a month before I was born. The kitchen became her kingdom as did that portion of the house that was attached to the kitchen, including Grandma's bedroom and the servants' bedrooms, as well as the spice and mushroom gardens, the lime tree, and the deep cool well. She rarely went into the main portion of the house. Grandma was called *Nyonya Besar*, or Grand Mistress, by the servants, while my mother was called *Nyonya Muda*, or Young Mistress. I wish you could feel how happy Grandma's kitchen was and see how well it was organized.

The kitchen where I was taught my first cooking lessons was two steps down from the rest of the house. The floor was not tile, but just hard-packed ground of red Java clay, because the stove was wood-burning and messy compared to modern stoves. The stove itself was brick, covered with white cement, and was built against the outside wall. It was actually a long counter with four round openings on top—the burners— and with four openings on the side which faced out into the kitchen where fires of four different temperatures could be built. The fire farthest to the left was usually built with wood and was used mostly for boiling rice or soup. The other fires were cooler and more even for simmering or warming and were usually built with charcoal. On top of the stove were two small charcoal barbecues. The smoke from the stove escaped into the air and then through air holes at the top of the wall where it met the sloping red-tile roof. The top two feet of the walls were open except for pieces of bamboo spaced about ten inches apart. On Java, one never has to worry about keeping a house warm unless one lives high in the mountains.

Next to the cement stove were large bamboo racks for drying the pots, pans, and dishes after they had been washed at the outdoor sink next to the well. Many woks hung from the ceiling, and against another wall were built bamboo and rattan shelves and spice cabinets. All of Grandma's spices were well organized and kept mostly in glass jars of many different sizes. They lined five long shelves, waiting like patient soldiers to add their flavors to the food. I believe now, as I did then, that the magic they brought to Grandma's food was due not only to her knowledge about them, but to her respect and love for them as God's great gift to the human race. Everyone knew that Grandma had a *tangan sedap*, or delicious hand, and that it was due to a power which was more than knowledge alone.

When I was first interested in cooking, I remember asking Grandma who it was that taught her to cook. Grandma just laughed. It was her happy Buddha-laugh and meant many things and nothing. I know she would laugh about my writing this to you. I hope that someday you will laugh about it, too, when you know how to cook.

First Lessons

MY FIRST LESSON

Because Depok was far in the countryside, there was no running water as in the city and, in fact, there is none today. Each home had a deep well at the side or back of the house and lifting the water, bucket by bucket, gave us all added respect for the gift of water. Depok wells have always been famous for good water. Hardly any mineral deposits are left in pots and pans and a Depoker's skin is unusually soft and clear.

Grandma saw to it that all cooking and drinking water was left standing outdoors overnight, covered with cheesecloth, to be enhanced by the night dew. The following day the water was brought indoors and placed in the large covered urn in the kitchen. Drinking water for the family was first boiled and then placed in the clay urn in the dining room, although the water was actually pure and clear right from the well. Each Friday when Bapak Jara, our Godfather, was with us, he would ask the blessing of the well and drop seven kinds of flowers into the water. Our well never went dry, even in the driest of years, and we sometimes shared with all our neighbors.

Grandma said that in order to be a cook I would have to learn to boil water and to do this I would first have to learn how to start a fire in the stove. After she had showed me how to place the wood, I was unsuccessful with about five matches and burnt my fingers as well. Finally, the wood caught fire and the smoke billowed up into my eyes. Grandma gave me a saucepan with water and told me to tell her when the water boiled. In spite of the tears in my eyes from the smoke, I watched the water with great interest and saw little bubbles form on the bottom of the pan and get bigger and bigger. It seemed to take forever for the water to come to a boil, and when the water finally rolled with big bubbles, I remember jumping up and down and yelling, "Grandma, look at that! Grandma, look at that!" Grandma gave me a pot holder and said, "Bring it here, Onie." When she had inspected it for ashes and smelled it, she said, "I'm sorry, child, but you'll have to do it over again because the water smells smoky." Grandma poured the water into another pan and added fresh water. In the meantime, the fire that I had started had almost turned to coals and was just right to cook on—the way it should have been when I first put on the pan.

That was how Grandma taught lessons. This time, the water seemed to come to a boil in only five minutes. Grandma was finally happy with the water and made me a cup of the most delicious tea that I have ever tasted. That was my first cooking lesson—boiling water. But even that wasn't so easy to do to meet Grandma's standards.

Grandma made sure that fresh water was left each day in the rice storeroom out of respect to Dewi Sri, and she always saved the water from cleaning fish for the garden plants.

KA

Ka was the first person who I cooked for regularly, so I should tell you about him. He was Grandma's good friend, and every Friday when he came visiting, he and Grandma could be seen talking together in Grandma's kitchen—Ka sitting close to the ground on the little three-legged stool that he always carried on his back, Grandma in her big rocking chair, rocking back and forth and laughing while she prepared dinner.

Ka was Chinese and appeared to be about fifty-eight years old. He had a flat-top haircut and was turning bald in the middle of his head. He had a curved back from carrying heavy loads of fabric on his shoulders as he went door to door taking orders and delivering the rolls of fabric that he wrapped in an unbleached linen sheet. Ka looked rather frightening to me when I was smaller. All of his bottom teeth were gold-capped, as were the two large front "horse teeth," which were the only ones he had left on top. I thought that he was about as ugly a man as I had ever seen.

Ka always dressed in an unbleached Nehru-style linen top with pants that came to just below the knees. His legs were so full of muscles from walking great distances that the veins were swollen on his bare calves. His shirt was usually open so that his navel showed, and you could see the string that held up his pants. He was a thrifty Chinese but he had a heart of gold. He didn't really mind when the Depok kids used to run after him, shouting, "Is your navel for sale, too?"

Everyone in Depok knew Ka as a door-to-door salesman and also as a walking bank. He was famous for lending out money at fifty percent interest. If someone was overdue on a loan, Ka just hung around their front yard until everyone knew what he was doing there and the borrower was shamed into paying.

On Fridays, after his regular rounds, he could always be found visiting Grandma and relaying gossip to her. It was my job to prepare Ka's tea because Grandma expected her oldest granddaughter to know how to be hospitable. I had to first boil the water, rubbing the smoke from my eyes, measure in the correct amount of tea, and then pour the boiling water into the teapot and set a teacup ready. Actually, it was more of a bowl that Ka drank from, Chinese style. He loved his tea boiling hot, with a piece of dark palm sugar to sweeten it. Ka and I became quite close as I grew older and he even loaned me money without telling my parents—they would have been ashamed to know their daughter borrowed money. Ka told me that he ate only broken rice and nothing else for five years when he first started his business. He later sent his oldest son to an expensive university.

PEELING ONIONS

Although I wasn't taught how to cook dishes right away, Grandma kept me busy doing all kinds of little jobs in the kitchen—peeling, chopping, and slicing vegetables in certain exact ways. For example, cucumbers had to be peeled from head to foot to have the best taste and not be bitter. Peeling onions had to be done properly, too. We called them onions, but they were Java onions, more like shallots. It was a hard job for a little girl because Grandma demanded that they be peeled perfectly. Grandma said that if I scarred onions with the knife while peeling them, I would someday marry a man with a pockmarked face. She was always telling me about the things I should and shouldn't do in order to marry a rich, handsome man. I remember asking her why she even bothered to teach me to cook if I was someday going to marry a rich man and have servants to do the cooking. Grandma laughed and said, "Well, let's just be prepared in case you marry a poor man. Then, at least, you will know how to cook." Grandma's "in case" turned out to be the way it was and I am forever thankful to her that I know how to cook. Her words are still in my ears.

TELUR PINDANG
Spiced Eggs

My second real lesson was how to boil a three-minute egg. I was told to wait until the big bubbles rose to the top of the water and then put in an egg. I then had to watch the sand timer and take the egg out when all the sand had passed through. It seemed easy enough, but I didn't get it right the first time because I forgot to put a long spoon in the water and the egg broke.

At Eastertime, Grandma always supervised the coloring of the Easter eggs, which took place two or three days before Easter. All the eggs were colored using natural ingredients. Green coloring was obtained by boiling eggs with the leaves of the *pandan wangie* bush, whose leaves were similar to lily leaves, but more fibrous. Red came from the bark of a certain tree whose name I no longer remember. But my favorite Easter eggs, which Grandma cooked throughout the year as well, were Pindang Eggs, dark brown inside as well as out and deliciously tasty.

Grandma liked to use duck eggs for Telur Pindang and she would sit for hours gently sanding the raw eggs with fine sandpaper to make the shells thin and porous. My brother Denny and I used to help with the sanding, but Denny had a hard time doing such fine handwork and usually broke all the eggs he tried to sand.

After thirty or so eggs were sanded, Grandma would boil them in a large, deep pan with salt, daun salam, lemon grass, chili peppers, asam, brown sugar, and onion peelings. I have made Pindang Eggs many times since, but the practice of sanding eggs, at least in our family, died with Grandma. I did not inherit her supreme patience. This is Grandma's recipe.

TELUR PINDANG

Spiced Eggs
Makes 1 dozen eggs

1 dozen eggs
2 tablespoons salt
2 leaves daun salam *curry leaves*
2 two-inch stalks sereh *lemon grass*
2 chili peppers (optional)
4 ounces *or* ¼ cup, well packed, peeled asam *tamarind*
2 tablespoons brown sugar
3 large handfuls onion skins (from approximately 10 onions)

Boil the eggs in water with spices for five minutes, or until hard. Peel the eggs and put them back in the spiced water and simmer for two hours. Serve hot or cold with rice.

If you want the eggs colored for hiding at Eastertime, do not peel, but let simmer for 24 hours, adding water when necessary.

daun salam
salam leaf: p. 90

sereh
lemon grass: p. 87

asam
tamarind: p. 86

WHITE RICE

My third lesson was more exciting because I was to learn something very important—how to cook rice in a pan. Grandma told me that after putting the rice in a pan, I should measure the water level with my forefinger, making sure that it was equal in volume to the amount of rice. She said that someday I would be able to judge the amount of water just by seeing the amount of rice. After rinsing the rice, I placed the pan on a high fire and waited until almost all the water had boiled away from the top of the rice. Then I covered the pan and moved it to a charcoal fire where it simmered. In about half an hour the rice was done perfectly and there was only the slightest crust on the bottom of the pan. I was so proud of my cooking and Grandma's compliments that I ran to the garden, picked fresh chili peppers, then gobbled down the rice flavored only with chili peppers and sweet soy sauce.

Of course, Grandma almost always steamed our rice in a steamer. Instead of covering the pan and cooking it that way, she would remove the partially cooked rice after the water had boiled from the top and place it in a steamer to finish cooking. That way no rice was lost in a bottom crust. But Grandma sometimes liked a crust for sizzling rice soup or for snacks and Poppie liked his rice cooked in a pan. If you cook rice in a pan and have a crust on the bottom (and if you didn't burn it), save the crust as Grandma did and let it dry out thoroughly for several days or even longer. Then break it in pieces about an inch square and fry it in oil. The rice will puff almost like popcorn and will have a delicious nutty taste. It can then be salted and eaten as a snack. If you want something sweet, you can melt brown sugar with a little water and a small amount of butter and pour it over the small squares after frying them. It's a healthy and inexpensive snack.

When taking rice from the storeroom, Grandma always put three portions of rice back into the storing container, out of respect for Dewi Sri. In that way, the container would always replenish itself. It was Grandma's way of thanking Nature and of showing respect to a certain living thing. Grandma said that a person who did not respect the source of the food being prepared for each meal would never be a great cook.

Although Grandma was raised in a wealthy Buddhist family, she preferred to live as an Indonesian and her beliefs were the same as most people who live all their lives in that country. She believed in one God that is all of Nature, each of whose vegetable, animal, or mineral families should be honored out of respect for the supreme intelligence of the universe. I am sure Grandma never ate an animal without thanking that particular family of beings, or cut a leaf from a plant without a respectful mind.

Grandma said that it was bad luck, financially, to burn rice, and that whistling near cooking rice would cause the nutrition of the rice to dissipate into the air, and no matter how much a person would eat, he would never be satisfied. (But maybe my whistling just irritated her.) I also learned very quickly that I must never step on rice that had fallen to the ground, but must pick it up and feed it to the animals or throw it away. It was a matter of respect for Dewi Sri as well as respect for the spirit of that place and those that had lived there before.

SAYUR SAPI
Beef Soup

My first real dish was vegetable soup made from a knucklebone base. For the most part, Grandma taught me *sayurs* first (soups, or vegetables served in a watery broth), then chili *sambals* (hot sauces), then fish dishes, and finally meat dishes. I thought that beef soup would be simple and that all I would have to do would be to cut up the vegetables and boil them together with the bone. But I was mistaken. Grandma said that the bone had to be boiled for at least two hours, until the eyes of the broth came to the surface of the water. Then the bone had to be taken from the water and the meat completely removed. The meat was then placed back into the boiling water with sliced vegetables to simmer. Then onions had to be sauteed in butter and added to the soup along with two tomatoes. It was then spiced with salt, pepper, and a little nutmeg. I was to guess the amount of spices necessary and then make adjustments. I had often watched Grandma when she spiced food and I was pleased with my taste. This is the recipe for my first soup, Sayur Sapi, or beef soup:

SAYUR SAPI

Beef Soup
Serves 4 to 6

8 cups water
1 large beef knucklebone
4 cups cut-up mixed vegetables (cabbage, potatoes, beans, carrots, etc.)
2 tomatoes, chopped
½ cup onions, chopped
1 tablespoon butter
2½ teaspoons salt
1½ teaspoons ground black pepper
½ teaspoon ground nutmeg
2 teaspoons chopped green onions
2 teaspoons bawang goreng

Boil the soup bone for at least two hours in water, then remove the meat from the bone. Place the meat and the vegetables in the cooking water. When the vegetables are tender, add the tomatoes and onions that have been sauteed in butter. Spice with salt, pepper, and nutmeg. Simmer until the vegetables are desired softness. Just before serving, add chopped green onions and bawang goreng to each individual bowl of soup.

bawang goreng
fried onions: p. 91

GARAM
Salt

Grandma said that garam, or salt, should always be added to food as the food was cooking. She would be shocked to see how most Westerners cook without salt, and then shake it on later at the table. Grandma was sure that uncooked salt, added to cooked food, was bad for the kidneys and the bladder, especially because it caused kidney stones. It would also be very impolite, and in fact insulting, to ask a Depok cook for more salt on food.

Some people may find it difficult to spice their food completely while it is cooking, but it just takes practice and the food tastes much, much better than adding spices later. You shouldn't call yourself a cook if you don't know how to salt food. In the ten years that I have had my restaurant in America, there have never been salt shakers on the tables. Whenever someone asks for salt (which is about once a year), I always leave the kitchen to find out if I've forgotten to add the salt. But it is almost always the case that the diner has just asked for salt out of habit, and hasn't yet tasted the food—usually the soup.

Salt is greatly respected in Indonesia. It is burned as an incense offering in the four corners of a room or at the four corners of a house. Or it may be tossed in the air in the four directions of the wind when a *dukun*, or holy person, wishes to communicate with the forces of Nature. If a Javanese villager travels from place to place, he always carries a small bag tucked into his sarong waist band. It contains the most necessary elements for survival: salt, to spice the food he can find or pick along the way; tea or coffee and raw sugar to sweeten it; and chili peppers for flavor. It is also bad luck to borrow salt after sunset—bad for the borrower and for the lender.

PERKEDEL GORENG
Fried Meatballs

My next formal lesson was Perkedel Goreng, or fried meatballs. I remember that it was difficult. First, Grandma had me wash four medium-sized potatoes very well and then boil them in the peel. After I determined that the potatoes were done by testing them with a bamboo stick, I had to take them from the water, peel them, and mash them, but not too smoothly, so that here and there there would be small lumps. To the mashed potatoes I was to add hamburger meat, which I had prepared by chopping meat with two cleavers over and over again. Then I had to add spices and mix in two eggs. Next, I had to bring about three-quarters of an inch of oil to the correct temperature in a frying pan. If a small slice of onion dropped into the oil rose to the top, the oil was the correct temperature.

Perkedel are delicious served as snacks or with steamed rice, and especially with vegetable soup. They also go well with white rice and Acar, or pickled vegetables. Perkedel Goreng have always been on the menu of my restaurant and are served hot from the frying oil, although they are quite good cold. They also add a different texture, their crispness contrasting nicely with white rice. With soup, try a bit of Perkedel with every fifth spoonful or so, and enjoy its crunch for variety.

Grandma said that there was nothing more important to know than which foods and spices went well together. She said that even if there were ten dishes for a meal, they all should complement each other perfectly in taste, texture, and color. This is my recipe for Perkedel Goreng:

PERKEDEL GORENG

4 medium potatoes
1 pound hamburger
1 tablespoon green onions
2½ teaspoons black pepper
1½ teaspoons garlic powder
2½ teaspoons salt
1 teaspoon nutmeg
6 or more eggs

Deep-Fried Meatballs
Serves 4 to 6

Boil potatoes until soft and then mash with hamburger, spices, and chopped onions, leaving some small lumps in the mashed potatoes. Mix about one-third of the mixture with two or three eggs until the dough-like raw Perkedel is just manageable enough to drop from a tablespoon into ¾-inch hot oil in a frying pan. When a small slice of onion dropped into the oil rises to the top, the oil is at the correct temperature. The consistency of the mixture can be varied to taste, some people preferring their Perkedel with a greater percentage of meat, others preferring more potatoes. Turn when one side is golden brown.

Care should be taken that the oil is not too hot, as the exterior may brown before the inside has had time to cook. It is best to test the first Perkedel by breaking it open to be sure it is done. In this case, it is better that the oil be cooler rather than hotter.

The oil should be changed occasionally. If the oil gets too fatty, from the cooking meat, it will bubble and froth so that the Perkedel is obscured from view. Practice will show you the ideal oil temperature. The entire bottom of the frying pan should be covered with Perkedel balls, as the temperature is then easier to maintain. While removing each batch of Perkedel, turn the heat down so that the oil doesn't heat up too much.

The Perkedel dough stores well for a day or two if the eggs haven't yet been added, so mix just enough for what will be cooked immediately.

SAYUR BAYEM
Spinach Sayur

This recipe originally came from Grandma's Chinese side of the family, but Grandma changed it slightly by adding terasi and lemon juice and leaving out the MSG. It is a vegetable dish to be served with white steamed rice and Perkedel Goreng, if you like.

SAYUR BAYEM

Spinach Sayur
Serves 4 to 6

4 tablespoons butter *or* 2 tablespoons cooking oil
½ onion, sliced
1 ripe tomato, chopped
1 leaf daun salam
2½ teaspoons salt
1 clove garlic, mashed
1 teaspoon terasi
2 cups chicken broth
corn from one cob
2 bunches spinach, chopped in two-inch lengths
½ teaspoon ground temu kunci (optional)
juice of 1 lemon

Saute in oil or butter the chopped onion, tomato, daun salam, salt, garlic, and terasi. When the onion is light brown, add the chicken broth and corn, and when the broth boils, add the spinach. When the spinach is almost done, sprinkle in the temu kunci and simmer for about five minutes until the spinach is tender. Squeeze in lemon just before serving.

daun salam   terasi   temu kunci: *p. 92*
salam leaf: p. 90   *shrimp paste: p. 89*

ACAR CAMPUR
Mixed Pickled Vegetables

In the 1930's in Depok, we never saw a vitamin label or talked about calories, but I have no doubt that Grandma balanced all of her meals according to the dietary needs of the whole family. At least three days every week she served pickled vegetables with dinner, and I remember asking her why she served them so often. Although they were delicious, I knew that it must have been for our health. Grandma said that the fresh turmeric root that colored the vegetables yellow was beneficial for the blood and kept a person's complexion healthy. The sour taste came from vinegar which was supposed to cleanse the body of unnecessary fat. The vegetables were just good for you, which everyone knew. Acar is especially tasty served with Perkedel Goreng, on sandwiches, with pot roasts, or with fish. It is too bad that fresh kunyit, or turmeric, is not available in markets here in America because the taste is incomparable, but ground kunyit is perfectly acceptable and much easier to obtain.

ACAR CAMPUR

Mixed Pickled Vegetables

5 or 6 kemiri *or* macadamia nuts *or* raw peanuts
2 cloves garlic
3 teaspoons salt
1 tablespoon kunyit
½ cup onion, chopped
1 leaf daun salam
1 two-inch length laos root *or* ½ teaspoon laos powder
1 two-inch stalk fresh sereh *or* ½ teaspoon dry sereh
2 cups white vinegar
1 cup hot water
1 cup green beans, French cut
1 cup carrots, shoestring sliced
2 cups white cabbage, shredded, *or* 2 cups bamboo
   shoots, sliced
1 cup cauliflower, sliced

Mash the candlenuts, garlic, salt, kunyit, and onion in a mortar. Saute all ingredients except vegetables and liquids in ¼ cup cooking oil until golden brown. Then add white sugar (not brown, as the vegetables will become soggy). Add white vinegar and hot water. Let the entire mixture come to a boil and then add the vegetables. Cook the vegetables briefly—usually just to the first boil, depending upon the type of vegetables used. It is important that the vegetables retain their crispness and it is better that they are undercooked rather than overcooked. May be served immediately, but it is best when chilled.

kemiri
candlenuts: p. 92

kunyit
turmeric: p. 89

daun salam
salam leaf: p. 90

laos
red ginger: p. 93

sereh
lemon grass: p. 87

Beancake, Bees,
and Beans

SAMBAL ULEK
Uncooked Hot Sauce

I will tell you a story about a type of food that you will probably never want to try and how your Uncle Denny and I learned to enjoy it.

One July, when I was about eleven and the rice was ready to be picked, I went with Nanny and Denny to Poppie's *sawah*, or wet rice fields, that were about a mile outside of Depok. We rode in *grobaks*, open carts made of rough lumber that had two huge wooden wheels and were pulled by *karbau*, water buffalo with long, curved horns. As we approached the rice fields, bumping along down the dirt road, I remember watching and wondering at the women standing knee deep in the muddy water of the rice paddies harvesting the rice. It was hard for me to understand how those women could endure the stifling heat and still sing happily as they worked. The sun was high in the sky, and heat, unmoved by even the slightest breeze, filled the valleys. I complained to Nanny that it was too hot to wait in the fields while the workers loaded the grobaks, so Nanny walked us to the nearest bamboo house in the village and asked permission for us to wait there.

Just as we arrived, several barefoot men wearing black cotton shorts were making torches by tying kerosene-soaked rags to the ends of bamboo poles. It seemed unusual to me that they were making torches in the middle of the day, so I watched them intently. One of the men asked Denny if he wanted to help them and when he answered that he did, they gave him a torch, and they all marched off. Several younger children and I followed at a distance until the men started climbing into a giant mango tree. It was then that I saw that they were interested in a large bees' nest that must have been at least two feet long and four feet around. One of the men saw me and the other children standing close by and waved us away, shouting, "You children get away from the tree. The bees will run amok. Hurry. Hurry!"

We all ran back to the house and watched from a distance as the men smoked out the bees' nest. The bees soon flew about like an angry cloud, and I remembered the time I almost died from bee stings. I shuddered as I watched Denny out there with just his torch for protection, but in a short while the men and Denny returned with the bees' nest. The smoke and flames had kept the bees away.

Several women broke open the nest and sat down on a mat on the dirt kitchen floor. Then, with tiny bamboo sticks, they pushed all the baby bees out of the nest, one at a time, into a large, clay bowl. Soon the bowl was filled with what looked to me like little fat white maggots, all squirming around on top of each other. They were rather nauseating, but it was apparent that they were going to be prepared as food.

The woman of the house, a pretty, middle-aged Javanese, who wore a spotless sarong and lace kebaya blouse, marinated the live baby bees in tamarind fruit that had been soaked in salt and water, treating the bugs gently to avoid squashing them. Then her oldest son picked a young papaya and started peeling it. The woman asked me if I would help by picking some lemon grass and chili peppers and when I walked to the rear of the house, I saw that there was an extensive vegetable and spice garden that was well cared for. I cut some lemon grass and picked the ripest chili peppers I could find, being careful to protect the stems so that the plant would produce all year long.

When the papaya soup was ready, Denny went to call Nanny. As I waited there, I thought about those village people who were so plain and who had so little, but who were happy and enjoyed being hospitable with the little they had. I also thought about all the wealthy Depok people I knew who could take a lesson from them.

When Nanny arrived, she went straight to the well and, as she washed her feet and hands, said to me, "Nonnie, are you behaving yourself?" As I told her how Denny and I had helped with the meal, I felt my stomach growling with hunger.

A woven reed mat was spread on the ground outside the kitchen and we all sat down, each with a clay bowl of papaya soup while sharing a stone mortar filled with a sambal of ground chili and shrimp paste. The rice was served from a woven bamboo basket with a wooden spoon, and I have never tasted better rice than the red-brown variety we were served that day. (At home, we always ate expensive long-grain white rice as Grandma preferred, but in Indonesia there are so many varieties of rice that one must be an expert to tell them all apart.) When the woman came from the kitchen with the deep-fried bees, they looked delicious, but I still remembered seeing them squirm around like little maggots and I was hesitant about eating them.

"Come on, Nonnie, sprinkle some on your rice," Nanny whispered in my ear. "You will insult these people if you don't eat their food."

I certainly didn't want to hurt the feelings of these people who had shared their food with us, so I sprinkled some of the bees on my rice, squeezed the rice between my fingers, and put it all in my mouth. I couldn't believe how good the bees tasted—crispy, sweet, and nutty on the outside and the inside soft like marshmallows. I looked over at Denny and he was eating like a starved man, scooping the rice and bees into his mouth with great gusto. He couldn't get enough.

After dinner we were served boiling-hot green tea that had been picked from the family's own tea bush. I asked the woman if I could take some bees for my Grandma and she smiled proudly at my request. She made a cone from a banana leaf, put in a big handful of bees, and then pinned it closed with a bamboo stick.

I will remember that hot sauce, papaya soup, red rice, and fried bees for as long as I live. I have never eaten fresher or better food. Nanny gave the village woman two silver half-gulden that she had taken from her waistband, and the woman was so happy that she kissed Nanny's hand, asking Allah's blessing for her.

When the rice had all been loaded in the grobaks in perfectly stacked bunches, and the carabao hitched in front, we were ready to start off down the dirt road. I wanted to give the woman something, too, and began to pull out one of the bunches of rice, but the foreman yelled at me that it would make the load uneven, so I asked the young boy on top of the load to throw me down two bunches which I gave the woman. The *mandur*, or foreman, told me not to forget to tell Poppie about my generosity, as Poppie would know exactly how much rice he should be receiving. Of each four bunches picked from the fields, Poppie received one and a half, the farmer one and a half, and the women harvesters one.

We had to walk in front of the grobak on the way home, and as we walked, Denny began teasing me about how the bees would come alive in my stomach while I slept and crawl out of my nose and mouth. I screamed and hit him with my fist until I hurt myself and Nanny had to intervene. She took my mind off the bees by stopping to buy young coconut with ice and syrup from a roadside stand.

When we got home, I went straight to the kitchen to find Grandma. I saw her sitting there, rocking back and forth in her chair, and I ran up to her. "Grandma, close your eyes and hold out your hand," I said. She did what I asked and when I had put the fried bees in her hand, I said, "Now put it in your mouth."

Grandma smiled, enjoying the game we often played. I could see immediately that Grandma liked the taste, and she said, "What is it?"

"I'll give you two guesses," I said.

"*Tekie*," she said, as she chewed away. (Tekie are small roots that are also prepared by deep-frying.)

"No," I said. "You are eating deep-fried maggots." I thought Grandma might get sick, but she started laughing so hard her whole huge body shook and shook. Finally she said, gasping for air, "Oh, you silly child. Of course I knew that they were baby bees. I'm not that dumb."

"Have you ever tasted them before, Grandma?" I asked, laughing.

"Not me," she said. "This was the first time. But I know that the villagers consider them a great delicacy. Remember, though, don't eat bees too often or you will get grey hair before your time."

I doubted that anyone would go to all the trouble to get bees and prepare them often enough to get grey hair, but it wasn't even two weeks later that Denny found a small bees' nest and he had me prepare deep-fried bees. Denny said that I made them even better than the village woman. Grandma never did believe in eating insects—she said it was because she had great respect for

their power and the damage they could bring to a house or crops if they came in great numbers.

There are two basic kinds of *sambals*, or hot sauces, in Indonesia: cooked and uncooked, or *ulek*, made entirely from uncooked chili peppers. This is the recipe for one type of sambal ulek that I copied from the village woman that day Denny and I first ate deep-fried bees.

SAMBAL ULEK

Raw Sambal

½ cup fresh green peppers, chopped (hot
    peppers optional)
¼ cup dry chili, crushed
2 teaspoons roasted terasi
½ teaspoon salt
2 teaspoons olive oil *or* sesame oil
juice of ½ lemon *or* 2 ½ teaspoons white vinegar

Grind peppers, chilis, terasi, salt, and oil in a mortar until
mixed to a rough paste, then add lemon juice or vinegar and
stir. Can be used on any rice dish.

terasi
shrimp paste: p. 89

TAHU GORENG
Deep-fried Beancake

Beancake was one of Grandma's favorites. After learning from Grandma about beancake, one of my bigger shocks when I went to Europe was seeing people buying and eating beancake raw—white, unappetizing, and with no taste at all. After coming to America, and realizing that so many people were interested in pure foods, I could see why people thought they might be eating food colorings if the beancake had color. But in Depok, we used only natural food colorings from roots, herbs, and leaves.

Grandma never allowed us to eat raw beancake because she said that it was bad for the teeth and stomach and caused worms, just as eating too many raw nuts would do the same thing. I don't know how true all of Grandma's beliefs were, but from my experience, most things were true. But let's get back to how to prepare beancake the proper way, Grandma's style. I should also mention that in Indonesia, salt is never added to the beancake as it will cause it to spoil sooner. Grandma said that she got this recipe from the beancake maker and salesman in Depok.

TAHU GORENG

Deep-fried Beancake
Serves 4

4 pieces beancake
½ teaspoon garlic powder
1 teaspoon salt
½ cup white vinegar *or* juice of 1 lemon
   or 2 tablespoons asam juice
2 tablespoons water
1 teaspoon kunyit

Soak the beancake in the above mixture for about half an hour. The beancake will then be firm and light yellow. Drain on a paper towel. Grease a frying pan with oil and fry the beancake on both sides until it is light golden brown and crispy. Serve with a sauce of lemon juice, kecap manis, and pepper. You can also cut the beancake into pieces and serve it topped with Bumbu Kacang (a peanut sauce, the recipe for which follows), a little kecap manis, lemon juice, and bawang goreng.

asam
tamarind: p. 86

kunyit
turmeric: p. 89

kecap manis
sweet soy sauce: p. 96

bawang goreng
fried onions: p. 91

BUMBU KACANG
Peanut Sauce

Peanut sauces are favorites of Indonesians, and are prepared in many different ways and served on many different kinds of foods, but especially barbecued meats and fowl. This Bumbu Kacang recipe comes from a taste that was made famous by an old couple who sold barbecued *sate kambing* (goat meat) at their roadside stand in Depok and who used this sauce over their meat. They were Grandma's friends and gave her the recipe that made their particular taste so unique. It is good over raw and cooked vegetables, meat, fowl, and as a dip for chips.

BUMBU KACANG

Peanut Sauce

4 cups roughly ground peanuts *or* 2 cups crunchy
   peanut butter
½ cup dark brown sugar
½ cup white vinegar
¼ cup kecap manis
1 teaspoon garlic powder
1 teaspoon powdered temu kunci
4 cups boiling water

Mix the ingredients in a double boiler, steamer, or on low
fire. Let simmer slowly, stirring until the sauce is smooth,
neither runny nor sticky.

kecap manis   temu kunci: *p. 92*
sweet soy sauce: p. 96

SAYUR ASAM PAPAYA MUDA
Young Papaya Soup

I remember Nanny saying to me one day, "Onie, do you want to go with me to the kampong? I have to check the coffee beans—they must be getting ripe." Grandma had a small piece of property far in the *kampong*, or jungle villages, near Depok. The property was about one and a half square acres with a small bamboo house, two papaya trees, and about twenty-four coffee bushes. Nanny's niece lived in the house and maintained the property in exchange for rent. When Grandma was younger she often went there in a horse-drawn carriage.

When Nanny and I arrived that day, I looked inside the one-room house and saw that it was little more than just a shack with a dirt floor, but it was neat and clean. Nanny's niece had a little boy and he was sent somewhere to get a bucket so that we could pick the coffee beans. There were many ripe coffee beans and the branches of the coffee bushes were full. The brightest red beans were already gone, though, because they had been eaten by the birds and the *luwak*, small furry squirrel-like animals with long tails.

As we were picking the coffee berries, I saw Nanny picking up the droppings of the luwak and putting them in a bucket. The droppings looked like small pieces of peanut brittle. I couldn't imagine why Nanny was picking them up. When I asked her, she told me that the droppings contain the best coffee beans in the world. Nanny explained how the luwak, which are very clean animals, eat only the ripest of the coffee berries. The meat is then digested in their stomachs and the seed, or bean, passes out of their bodies. Whereas coffee berries picked by humans are in many stages of ripeness, the berries picked by the luwak are only the ripest, most mature. When luwak beans are washed clean and roasted, they are considered the best coffee beans possible and bring the highest prices. They are such a delicacy that they are not exported. Some villages actually raise luwak to "harvest" the coffee.

The husband of Nanny's niece was just a village carpenter and quite poor, so when lunchtime came we ate a plain meal of young papaya soup from the trees on the property. We also had dark red rice that Nanny's niece had earned by working in the rice paddies. The green papaya soup was delicious—tangy from the tamarind and hot from fresh chili peppers. There were also fish patties, made of small minnows from the nearby stream that had been molded with egg and dried flowers, then fried in coconut oil.

This is the recipe for the green papaya soup we ate that day. You can also substitute a vegetable called chayote that is sold in many Mexican markets or even zucchini or squash.

SAYUR ASAM PAPAYA MUDA

Young Papaya Soup
Serves 4 to 6

2 medium young papaya *or* a medium chayote
   or 4 small zucchini *or* cucumbers
2 fresh chili peppers, sliced
½ teaspoon terasi
1 two-inch stalk fresh sereh *or* 1 teaspoon dry sereh
2½ teaspoons salt
½ onion, chopped
2 ounces *or* 4 tablespoons peeled asam with seeds *or*
   juice of 1 lemon
2 teaspoons brown sugar
1 leaf daun salam
3½ cups water
2 tablespoons cooking oil *or* 1 tablespoon butter

Bring the water to a boil, then add all the ingredients except
the asam and papaya. When the water boils again, add the
papaya and the asam. Simmer to desired softness for the
papaya or vegetable.

terasi   **sereh**   **asam**
shrimp paste: p. 89   *lemon grass: p. 87*   *tamarind: p. 86*

daun salam
salam leaf: p. 90

CA BUNCIS
Crispy Green Beans

My grandchildren, your Grandma just came back from the supermarket where I saw the most beautiful fresh green beans. They reminded me of how often, just after the Second World War, when food was scarce, we ate a green bean dish from a recipe of my Nanny's. Nanny was a devout Moslem woman in her seventies who helped raise my two brothers and me. She was treated just like a member of our family and slept in Grandma's room. Her recipe is excellent if you have to live on a tight budget or if you are a vegetarian. I think the recipe is a mixture of Chinese and Indonesian cooking, but mostly it is a family recipe.

CA BUNCIS

Crispy Green Beans
Serves 4 to 6

1 pound green beans, French cut
2 tablespoons butter (Grandma preferred butter, but
   1 tablespoon oil is all right to use)
½ onion, sliced
1 clove garlic, mashed or pressed
1 teaspoon black pepper
1 teaspoon salt
¼ cup kecap manis
½ cup water

Saute all the ingredients, except liquids, in a wok over a
high fire, stirring quickly until the beans start to soften, but
are still crispy. Add water and cover for about five minutes.
Then add kecap manis and serve with white steamed rice,
noodles, or potatoes. You may also add leftover pieces of
ham, bacon, or chicken, and fresh corn or spinach.

kecap manis
sweet soy sauce: p. 96

Depok 1945

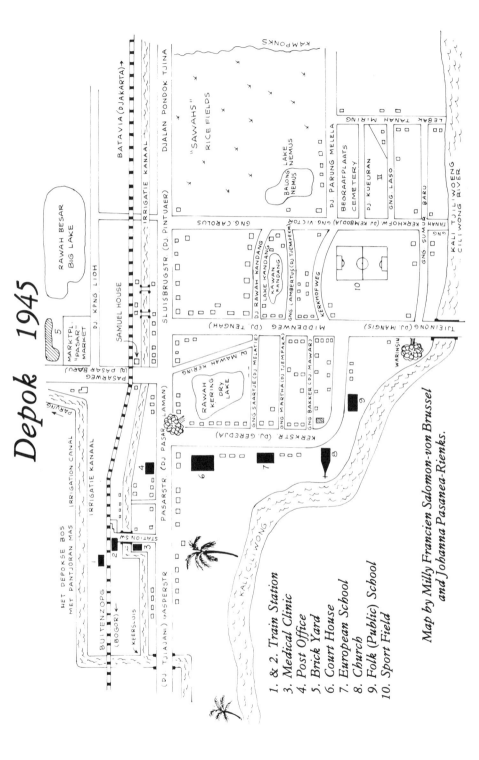

1. & 2. Train Station
3. Medical Clinic
4. Post Office
5. Brick Yard
6. Court House
7. European School
8. Church
9. Folk (Public) School
10. Sport Field

Map by Milly Francien Salomon-von Brussel
and Johanna Pasanea-Rienks.

RAWAH BESAR
BIG LAKE

BATAVIA (DJAKARTA) →

DJALAN PONDOK TJINA

KAMPONGS

"SAWAHS"
RICE FIELDS

BALONG LAKE
NEMUS NEMUS

DJ PARUNG MELELA

BEGRAAFPLAATS
CEMETERY

DJ KUEURAN

GNG LASO

GNG SUMUR BARU

LEBAK TANAH MIRING

KALI TJILIWOENG
CILIWONG RIVER

IRRIGATIE KANAAL

DJ KPNG LIOH

SAMUEL HOUSE

MARKTPL.
"PASAR"
MARKET

SLUISBRUGSTR (DJ PINTUAER)

GNG CAROLUS

KERKHOFW (DJ KEMBODJA) GNG VICTOR

GNG
TANAH

PASARWEG
(2) PASAR BARU

PASARSTR (DJ PASAR LAMAN)

MAWAH KERING

RAWAH
KERING
DRY LAKE

DJ RAWAH KANDANG

LAKE KANDANG

KAWAN
KANDANG

GNG LAMBERTUS (DJ TOEMPENG)

KERKHOFWEG

MIDDENWEG (DJ TENGAH)

GNG SAARTJE (DJ MELATIE)

GNG MARTHA (DJ TJEMPAKA)

GNG BAKKER (DJ MAWAR)

KERKSTR (DJ GEREDJA)

TJIEINONG (DJ MANGIS)

WARINSIN

WARINSIN

HET DEPOKSE BOS
MET PANTJORAN MAS
IRRIGATION CANAL
IRRIGATIE KANAAL

PARUNG

BUITENZORG
(BOGOR) →

KEERSLUIS

(DJ TJIAJANI) JASPERSTR

STATION SW

KALI CILIWONG

OMA LIES

Oma Lies was another person I remember well from my childhood. Although she wasn't blood family, she was considered a family member. *Oma* means grandmother and is a respectful way of addressing any older woman who could be a grandmother. *Lies* is short for Elizabeth. Oma Lies was one of my many cooking teachers. Her specialities were food spiced with chili peppers because Padang people like their food chili pepper hot.

Oma Lies was my Grandma's good friend and came from Padang, on the island of Sumatra. She married Oom, or Uncle, Johan who was a pure Depoker. She was a big woman with a large nose and two big front teeth which were black-red from chewing betel nut. She had only one foot having lost the other to diabetes. We used to laugh because Oma Lies was always ordering her husband around while she sat back and waited to be served. She knew that we all laughed, but she felt she deserved the service, and I guess she did.

Oma Lies was then about sixty-eight years old and lived with Oom Johan on twenty acres of land. Their house was surrounded by pineapple plants and pistachio trees. They also had a barn and Dutch milk cows whose milk was sold at the market. No one dared trespass on Oma Lies' land because poisonous snakes, black with orange stripes, lived in the pineapple fields and Oma Lies used to talk to them. Oma Lies' house was immaculate, with a kitchen floor you could eat off of.

Oma Lies used to tell me that to be a good cook, a person also had to be a good buyer of food, and I remember that once Oma Lies had me go to the market for her. I was only about ten years old then, and I thought I was smart enough to cheat her—but it was the last time I tried.

One day, when I was visiting with my mother, Oma Lies asked me to go shopping for her because her maid hadn't come to work. She needed fresh ciri leaf to chew with her betel nut and a carp for dinner. I looked forward to watching her prepare it.

Oma Lies' house was about six blocks from the market, and I had to cross the railroad tracks to get there. When I came to the street that crossed the tracks, I saw my brother, Denny, riding his bicycle. "Where are you going, Denny?" I called. "Please take me to the market, I'm tired of walking. I have to shop for Oma Lies."

I changed my voice to sound like Oma Lies and said, "Go get my spittoon. Go get my cane. Go get me some lemonade." By imitating Oma Lies, I soon had Denny laughing so hard that, as we were riding along, he almost got into an accident with a karbau cart that was coming down the hill from the market. Anyway, I bought the best fish and ciri leaves that I could find. When I returned to her house, Oma Lies inspected all the items carefully and methodically, looking inside the mouth of the fish to see that it was bright red, and checking each ciri leaf to be sure it was fresh and had no spots. Finally, she said, "I have some change coming."

I had planned to cheat Oma Lies out of ten cents, and had given her that much less in change. "Leonie, don't try and lie to me," she said. I looked into my mother's eyes, trying to show no expression. Mommie didn't say anything but she probably assumed the worst, because at that age I was often very *brandal*, or bratty.

"I know exactly what you have been doing," Oma Lies said. "Close to the railroad station you saw your brother Denny and you started making fun of me by saying, *Go get my spittoon. Go get my cane. Go get me some lemonade.* And my ciri leaf and fish cost only 2.75, not 2.85."

I just shrugged my shoulders. I didn't want to let her know that I was impressed. "Oh well," I said. "I just wanted to try."

Oma Lies didn't particularly like kids, but I knew that she liked me. We enjoyed each other. I thought that someday I would like to be able to do the things Oma Lies did. You see, because of her strong mind, everyone considered Oma Lies to have powerful magic. Years later, after I married, we became close friends and she told me many things about her ''magic.'' But that is another story.

IKAN PEPES
Wrapped Fish

After my twelfth birthday, I was allowed to cook whatever two dishes I desired for the Saturday family dinner. Ikan Pepes was one of my favorite dishes to make and the first fish dish that I ever cooked. Grandma was so proud when I first made it, and I was, too, because it came out so well that it became my father's favorite. I had to cook it that way for him all the time. This is the way I prepare it now. Of course I substitute aluminum foil for the banana leaf most of the time, even though some flavor is lost. This recipe is good for ulcer patients and weightwatchers.

IKAN PEPES

Wrapped Fish
Serves 2

1 pound fish filet *or* 2 ten-inch trout
2 teaspoons salt
2 tablespoons fresh peeled asam *or* juice of 1 lemon
1 tablespoon cooking oil
1 tomato, sliced
½ onion, sliced
2 cloves garlic, sliced
1 leaf daun salam
5 fresh mushrooms, sliced
1 tablespoon dry sereh *or* 1 two-inch stalk fresh sereh,
  sliced lengthwise
1 tablespoon green onions, chopped

Rub the fish with salt, oil, and asam. Then place all the
ingredients in a banana leaf or aluminum foil and roast on a
charcoal fire or place in a 350° oven for about 45 minutes or
until done.

asam	**daun salam**	**sereh**
tamarind: p. 86	*salam leaf: p. 90*	*lemon grass: p. 87*

SAYUR LODEH
Vegetables in Coconut Juice

I always thought it unusual that my mother and grandmother, who were Chinese, preferred Indonesian cooking, especially dishes cooked with chili peppers, while my father, who was Indonesian, preferred Chinese cooking. However, my mother didn't care too much for vegetables cooked in *santan*, or coconut juice, but Grandma did, and almost every week we were blessed with Grandma's famous Sayur Lodeh. Here is the recipe:

SAYUR LODEH

Vegetables in Coconut Juice
Serves 4 to 6

4 or 5 kemiri *or* macadamia nuts
3 teaspoons salt
1 teaspoon terasi
2 cloves garlic
2½ cups boiling water
1 large onion, chopped
1 two-inch length laos root *or* ½ teaspoon laos powder
   (optional)
1 green chili pepper, cut in half (optional)
6 cups mixed vegetables, such as green beans cut in
   one-inch lengths, corn cut from the cob, shredded white
   cabbage, bamboo shoots, carrots, etc.
4 cups santan

Mash the kemiri, salt, terasi, and garlic and then add to the
boiling water along with the onion, laos and chili pepper.
Add the vegetables. When they are tender, add the santan
and serve just before it boils again.

kemiri	terasi	laos
candlenuts: p. 92	*shrimp paste: p. 89*	*red ginger: p. 93*

santan
coconut juice: p. 94

HAM & CHEESE MACARONI

I want to give you the next recipe because it was a favorite of all your parents when they were young. It is not an Indonesian or Chinese recipe, but a European-style casserole. It was given to my Grandma by her girlfriend who was married to a Dutchman, the head cook of the Governor of Indonesia. Of course his name has long been forgotten—even Grandma couldn't remember it.

HAM & CHEESE MACARONI

Serves 4 to 6

1 pound elbow or pipe macaroni
¼ pound butter
1 cup cooked ham, shoestring sliced
2 cups milk
1 pound sharp cheddar cheese, grated
6 eggs
2 teaspoons ground black pepper
1 teaspoon salt
dash ground nutmeg

Boil the macaroni in salted water, drain, and rinse in cold running water. Reserve 1 tablespoon of the butter to grease a casserole dish; melt remaining butter in a skillet. Add the cooked ham, milk, half the cheddar cheese, and the pepper, salt, and nutmeg. Break in the eggs and mix all together. Simmer slowly on a low fire, stirring constantly. After the mixture thickens, pour half into the buttered casserole dish, add a layer of half the remaining cheese, then add the rest of the cooked mixture, and top with the remaining cheese. Bake in a 350° oven until golden brown. The ideal is to have the top slightly crispy and the inside still moist. I often saw it served as a *rijsttaffel* dish, but it is good by itself.

AYAM PANGGANG
Barbecued Chicken

My wish, my grandchildren, is that one of you will grow up to enjoy the art of cooking and someday be able to cook all of the recipes that I have learned from around the world. The next recipe's origins are not known—it has just always been cooked in our family. It is called Ayam Panggang, or barbecued chicken Indonesian-style. If you don't like hot food, leave out the chili pepper—it will still be delicious. It should be served with white steamed rice or buttered egg noodles, if you prefer.

AYAM PANGGANG

Barbecued Chicken
Serves 2 to 4

1 whole frying chicken, cut in half
2 cloves garlic, crushed
1 ounce fresh ginger, grated
1 ounce fresh ginger, crushed
juice of 3 lemons
4 tablespoons butter
1 teaspoon black pepper
2 cloves
½ cup kecap manis
2 tablespoons water
1 tablespoon crushed dry chili pepper (optional)

Cut the chicken in half lengthwise, then rub with the crushed cloves of garlic and the grated ginger. Squeeze the juice of one lemon over the chicken, then set the chicken aside and let it stand for thirty minutes. Barbecue the chicken over a charcoal fire.

While the chicken is cooking, prepare a sauce by melting the butter in a saucepan, then adding juice of two lemons, black pepper, chili pepper, cloves, and crushed ginger. Simmer from three to five minutes and then add kecap manis and water.

When the chicken is done, pound lightly with a mallet so that the meat fibers separate; in this way, the sauce which is now reheated and poured over the chicken will be absorbed.

I think Ayam Panggang is even better the following day when the spices have entirely soaked into the chicken. It is good cold, too, and will keep well in the ice box.

kecap manis
sweet soy sauce: p. 96

SAYUR TUMIS
Cucumber Soup

Indonesians almost always enjoy a watery soup with each meal—not before, but during the meal. I think Sayur Tumis goes very well with Ayam Panggang. This is the recipe:

SAYUR TUMIS

Cucumber Soup
Serves 2 to 4

2 cloves fresh garlic, sliced
2 tablespoons sesame oil
6 dried shrimp
½ chopped onion
½ teaspoon salt
½ teaspoon black pepper
4 thin slices fresh ginger
2 cups chicken broth
½ ounce dry beanthread
2 green onions, chopped
2 cucumbers, peeled and cubed

Saute the spices in oil, add broth, and when it boils, add the cucumber and allow to simmer for about ten minutes. Don't overcook the cucumbers, or they will be bitter.

beanthread
thin soy noodles, found in Oriental groceries and gourmet section of supermarket

PERKEDEL BAKAR
Indonesian Meatloaf

I loved to go to wedding parties with Grandma, because she was usually chosen as one of the head cooks for those celebrations. Two of the other head cooks were usually my great aunts. Grandma took me along to cut vegetables and bring her the things she needed. Of course in those days there were no birth control pills and the smaller families had five children while the larger ones had fourteen or fifteen. That is why there were usually ten or twelve wedding parties every year.

All the weddings were different, some very large if the families were wealthy. I remember one of the biggest weddings—one of Poppie's nieces, Francien, was to be married to the son of the president of Depok. Grandma, my great aunts Pauline and Sophia, and three other ladies were to be the head cooks. All of the cooks were almost as large as Grandma and were the best in Depok.

Poppie donated bamboo from our bamboo jungle and workers were kept busy cutting it for several days. Carpenters and plasterers built a temporary kitchen and dining room that was added on to the main kitchen with extra stoves, open walls, and a roof of coconut fronds. Everyone was busy because the custom was for all the friends and relatives to lend a hand. Some donated coconuts, others fresh fruit, rice, sugar, coffee, tea, fish, or just labor. Tables were made from wood and bamboo and chairs were rented from the church.

When the day of the wedding came, Grandma couldn't walk the three blocks to Francien's house and was picked up by horse cart. I was permitted to go early with Grandma, to carry her box of extra-sharp knives, her cigars, betel nuts, and *ciri* leaves. When we arrived at Francien's, I saw that the other head cooks were already there ordering about the servants from several households.

The first item of business was to kill the animals and butcher them. A two-hundred-pound pig was first. It was put in a large woven rattan cone so that the head stuck out, and placed on a table. The butcher gave thanks to God for the right to kill the pig, and asked a blessing of the pig. With the struggling pig held on top of the table, the butcher severed the main vein in the neck and blood spurted out. The first half pint or so was allowed to run into the ground as a tribute to the Earth, and the remainder was caught in a bucket that had salt in it. The blood congealed immediately and formed a big blood cake. The blood cake was then sliced in one-inch thick squares, marinated in garlic, salt, fresh tamarind, and then fried. Fried blood has a delicious taste that is difficult to describe, but I think most westerners might find the whole idea too unusual, anyway.

After all the animals had been killed, including one calf, two goats, and about one hundred chickens, the people who worked for the party ate the blood, stomach, and intestines. The intestines were first washed, then boiled, spiced, skewered on bamboo sticks, and barbecued.

Big wood fires were built and special workers carried wood and kept the fires going. There were also water carriers who supplied all the cooks, and one person who did nothing but bring refreshments to the cooks such as soft drinks, beer, coffee, or tea.

Grandma cooked a one-hundred gallon drum of split pea soup with a pork bone base that day. It is this particular recipe that I copied for the daily soup in my restaurant. One of Grandma's speciality dishes which she was also to prepare was Indonesian meatloaf, called Perkedel Bakar.

I remember Grandma sitting in her chair alongside a table ordering me and the servants about, laughing and joking with everyone. I also remember the sound of Grandma's cleavers on the wooden chopping block. It was like music to me—tok, tok, tok—like drums in the distance. Grandma chopped about ten pounds of pork and beef which would make twenty meatloaves.

Some of the meatloaf pans were clay and some were aluminum. I remember having to bring Grandma a large clay mixing bowl that she put the meat into. It was so large that I almost couldn't carry it. I then had to peel about fifty potatoes which Grandma mashed in with the meat, chopped onions, garlic, milk, and spices. Grandma spooned the mixture into the meatloaf pans, sticking in whole cloves all over the top. I then had to carry the pans of meatloaf to the ovens at the fires. Each oven was actually a large drum that had four legs attached at the bottom and a lid with a raised edge. After the pans were placed inside, the fire heated the oven from below and charcoal was placed on the lid so there was even heat all around. A large handle on top allowed the lid to be removed with a wooden stick without disturbing the charcoal. The Perkedel dishes were placed inside and baked until the tops were golden brown.

When Grandma served the Perkedel Bakar, it was always with her special sauce. The sauce was made by heating butter, sweet soy sauce, and lemon juice in a saucepan, and was then poured boiling hot on top of the Perkedel Bakar just as it was served.

At about four in the afternoon, all the family and friends went to the church for the wedding ceremony which lasted about an hour. The bride and groom were the only ones who rode in an automobile—everyone else walked or went in horsecarts. Before the ceremony ended, ten or twelve friends ran back to the house to receive the bride and groom and throw rice. While a local orchestra played a tune similar to *Here Comes The Bride*, champagne glasses were set on the table for the toasts. As I remember, over five hundred persons sat down to dinner that day, the children at separate tables. The dinner had about twenty-four courses and lasted until two in the morning with dancing going on the entire time. I was glad to be a kid then, and to be able to sit with the other children because at the big table it seemed as if there were a thousand speeches and toasts. Even the departed members of the bride's and groom's families were not forgotten. On the following day, the bride and groom took all the flowers from the wedding to the graveyard and offered them to the departed family members, asking their blessing for the marriage.

It was the custom for each of the head cooks to take home the leftover food, and some of them were so greedy that they took enough food to feed a whole neighborhood. Grandma just took food that was her grandchildren's favorite. After that wedding, my Grandma was so tired that I had to massage her big fat legs every day. Poor Grandma. She still loved to cook for everyone, even though she couldn't do that much. Everything had to be put in front of her, close by where she could reach it.

The wedding gave the women and girls of Depok something to talk about at their teas, and served as a place where teenagers could have their first "date." For several weeks after the wedding, there would be gossiping about everyone and everything.

About a month after that wedding, Grandma let me make my first Perkedel Bakar. This is a recipe that I use now, which has smaller portions, of course. Perkedel Bakar has always been one of your parents' favorite dishes and is good for stretching a food budget—as I found out in Holland when times were hard after the war, and when we first came to this country. Perkedel Bakar can also be eaten cold with hot rice or sliced and eaten on bread. Here, my grandchildren, is your great-great-grandmother's recipe.

PERKEDEL BAKAR

Indonesian Meatloaf
Serves 4 to 6

4 medium potatoes, boiled
½ pound lean ground beef
½ pound coarsely ground pork
1½ teaspoons salt
1 teaspoon pepper
½ teaspoon ground nutmeg
1½ cups milk
4 eggs
12 whole cloves

Mash the potatoes and meat along with salt, pepper, and nutmeg. Mix in four eggs and milk. Spoon into a loaf pan, smooth the top, and stud with whole cloves. Bake in oven at 350° for about half an hour until the top is golden brown.

Sauce

¼ pound butter
¼ cup kecap manis
juice of 1 lemon
¼ cup water

Just before serving, melt butter and kecap manis in a saucepan. When the butter melts, add water and lemon juice. When the sauce froths, pour over meatloaf and serve.

kecap manis
sweet soy sauce: p. 96

COOKING FOR THE DEPARTED

On Java, a cook often cooks for those relatives or friends who have passed on. However, the food is not set aside as if it were an offering (except on birthdays), but is eaten by all. More than anything else, it is a way of remembering someone who was loved. Whenever I cook my Grandma's, father's, mother's, or brothers' favorite dishes, I always remember them in my thoughts and mentally offer them a taste.

Another Javanese superstition is that if food is dropped or spilled on the floor, it may be that someone wanted to taste that food and was not remembered when it was cooked or eaten. Or the accident may be attributed to the spirit of the particular kitchen or dining room. Such occurrences provide the opportunity for everyone to guess and laugh about which spirits may have wanted to taste that particular food. Javanese families are very close, even in death. In fact, there is no death in Indonesia as most western people think of it.

OPOR AYAM
Chicken Cooked in Coconut Juice

I remember that this chicken dish was usually served on birthdays or on Sundays. The recipe came originally from Semarang, Middle Java. My uncle lived there for many years, and when he returned to Depok, he brought his cook. We all called her *Ibu Iyum*, or Mother Iyum. This is the recipe I copied from her for Opor Ayam.

OPOR AYAM

Chicken Cooked in Coconut Juice
Serves 4 to 6

1 whole frying chicken, cut up
1 large onion, chopped
4 cloves garlic, finely sliced
4 or 5 kemiri *or* macadamia nuts
1 tablespoon ground coriander
1 tablespoon cumin
½ tablespoon ground black pepper
3 teaspoons salt
1 two-inch piece ginger
2 cups water
1 tablespoon cooking oil
2 three-inch stalks sereh
　　or 2 teaspoons dry sereh
2 leaves daun salam
½ cup lemon juice
1 teaspoon kencur powder
4 cups santan

Mash the onion fine along with garlic, kemiri, coriander, cumin, pepper, and salt, then flatten the ginger and add entire mixture to boiling water. Rub the chicken well with the cooking oil, and when the water has boiled again, place the chicken in along with the sereh, daun salam, kencur, and lemon juice. Boil until tender. When the chicken is the desired tenderness, add the santan and bring almost to a boil, but do not allow to boil. Serve immediately.

kemiri	sereh	daun salam
candlenuts: p. 92	*lemon grass: p. 87*	*salam leaf: p. 90*
kencur: *p. 92*	**santan**	
	coconut juice: p. 94	

NASI UDUK
Rice Cooked in Coconut Juice

When I was young, I always used to look forward to my birthday because on birthdays Grandma cooked her grand-children's favorite foods. Mine was Nasi Uduk, and all the special dishes that went along with it. Nasi Uduk is just a special way to cook rice and it is usually reserved for special occasions. Although it is meant to be eaten with other dishes—Perkedel Goreng is one—it is good just by itself because of the toppings that go with it. Nasi Uduk is prepared differently in each family. This is the way Grandma made it.

NASI UDUK

Rice Cooked in Coconut Juice
Serves 4 to 6

6 kemiri *or* macadamia nuts
3 cloves garlic
2 teaspoons black pepper
4 cups water
1 leaf daun salam
1 two-inch length ginger
1 two-inch stalk fresh sereh *or* 1 teaspoon dry sereh
1 tablespoon salt
4 whole cloves
2 pounds long grain rice
4 cups santan

Grind the kemiri with garlic and pepper and add to the water along with the daun salam, ginger, sereh, salt, cloves, rice, and santan. Boil until all the liquid is gone, stirring constantly, and then place the rice in a steamer and cook until fluffy.

Serve the rice hot on a platter, decorated with a topping of bawang goreng, strips of egg omelet, slices of red chili (hot or mild), and slices of raw cucumber. The Nasi Uduk hot sauce is served alongside the rice in a separate dish, and it is made like this:

kemiri	daun salam	sereh
candlenuts: p. 92	*salam leaf: p. 90*	*lemon grass: p. 87*
santan	bawang goreng	
coconut juice: p. 95	*fried onions: p. 91*	

Sauce:

½ cup ground dry chili peppers
1 teaspoon terasi
½ cup roasted peanuts *or* ¼ cup crunchy peanut butter
1 teaspoon salt
½ cup white vinegar
2 teaspoons white sugar

Mash the chilis, terasi, peanuts, and salt in a mortar. Then mix with vinegar and sugar until smooth, leaving the peanuts slightly crunchy.

terasi
shrimp paste: p. 90

NASI GORENG
Indonesian Fried Rice

One of the most important days of the year in Depok was June 28th. On that day each year there was a celebration in honor of the birthday of Cornelius Chastelein, the founder of Depok. Almost all the Christian churches on Java came to Depok for a huge convention. Each church was represented by its minister, some of the congregation, and at least one of its choirs. Many of the choirs sang in harmonies typical of the different Indonesian islands, such as Ambon or the Moluccas. The choirs sang all day and into the night. The Depok church had six different choirs comprised of different ages and types of voices. There were also sporting events for the boys and young men such as climbing a soaped pole for prizes at the top.

Chastelein's birthday was an especially big day for Depokers because of the food stands that many families set up in the area surrounding the church. The property was about the size of two soccer fields with packed red dirt ground and giant *duku* fruit shade trees scattered about. I guess that there must have been about fifty different food stands selling cold beer, lemonade, home-made ice cream, candies, and whatever food specialities anyone had. I think my father's stand was always the most popular and profitable. (Of course, ten percent of all sales went to the Depok church.)

I was always excited when I saw Poppie preparing his own recipe for Nasi Goreng, or fried rice, for the stand. I should tell you that Nasi Goreng, which is known throughout the world as an Indonesian dish, isn't really. Fried rice is actually a Chinese dish which the Dutch colonists liked so well that they included it in their *rijsttaffel* feasts. Indonesian villagers usually don't eat fried rice because it is believed that burning rice, or having it pop when frying, is disrespectful to Dewi Sri. I will never forget how mad Grandma would get if even one grain of rice was dropped in the fire. And even though she was Chinese, Grandma wouldn't fry rice, except occasionally for breakfast when we were out of other food, and then she fried it very lightly mixed with eggs. But let me get back to Poppie's Nasi Goreng stand.

Poppie prepared his fried rice by first steaming the rice and then cooling it on a bamboo tray. In the meantime, green onions were chopped and placed in a large bowl. Egg omelets were fried and sliced into thin strips, as were pieces of ham, and then added to the bowl. Mounds of bawang goreng were also prepared, and candlenuts were ground in a mortar with garlic. I was permitted to help by peeling boiled shrimp and removing crab meat from the shell. Poppie always kept his cooking oil in an unmarked bottle, and I didn't find out until I was fourteen years old that he used the finest quality imported sesame oil for his Nasi Goreng. It gave the fried rice a distinctive taste because most people did not cook with sesame oil—it was Poppie's secret ingredient for fried rice.

On Chastelein's birthday, the temporary brick stoves were already in place with three holes for the wood fires and the giant woks. Poppie did all the cooking with an assistant, a dishwasher, and two waiters who waited on a long, long table with bamboo benches that would seat between seventy-five and one hundred people. The tables were covered with white linen tablecloths and everything looked very elegant among the beautiful fruit trees with their small, thick, velvety dark-green leaves.

I was too young to help much with all the frantic activity that went on at Poppie's stand, but I enjoyed whatever I could do to help. And I was so proud when I heard the compliments for Poppie's food. Although he was an Indonesian, Poppie loved Chinese food and he went to great lengths to learn from all the best Chinese cooks. Then he added his own special touches. Here is Poppie's recipe for Nasi Goreng:

NASI GORENG

Indonesian Fried Rice
Serves 4 to 6

2 kemiri *or* macadamia nuts
2 teaspoons salt
2 cloves garlic
2 tablespoons sesame oil
½ cup ground pork
½ medium onion, finely chopped
4 tablespoons shrimp, chopped
2 tablespoons crab meat
2 eggs
5 cups cooked rice
2 tablespoons kecap manis
1 tablespoon kecap manis *or* regular soy sauce
  or fish-flavored soy sauce

Topping:
2 tablespoons green onions, chopped
2 tablespoons ham pieces, matchstick sliced
2 tablespoons bawang goreng

Mash the kemiri, salt, and garlic in a mortar. Then place in a wok or frying pan and saute in sesame oil until light brown. Add the ground pork, onion, shrimp, and crab, stirring constantly. When the pork meat is done, break in eggs and scramble lightly until done, and then add rice, mixing all together. If the egg is not entirely cooked, it will stick to the rice and spoil it, in my opinion, although some people seem to like it that way. When all the ingredients are well mixed through the rice, mix in the soy sauces. Before serving, top with the above topping ingredients and slices of egg omelet.

kemiri	kecap manis	bawang goreng
candlenuts: p. 92	*sweet soy sauce: p. 96*	*fried onions: p. 91*

ACAR KETIMUN
Cucumber Salad

My father also served a cucumber salad with his Nasi Goreng because the tastes and textures went so well together. This is the recipe for Poppie's Acar Ketimun:

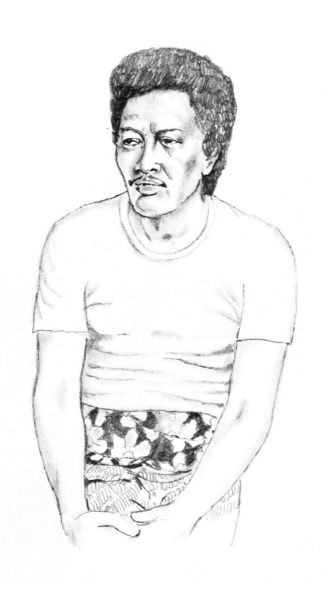

ACAR KETIMUN

Cucumber Salad

2 firm young cucumbers, cubed
½ medium onion, sliced
½ cup white vinegar
1 tablespoon oil
1½ teaspoons salt
1 teaspoon pepper
juice of 1 clove fresh garlic *or* ½ teaspoon garlic powder
½ tablespoon white sugar

Let the onion and cucumber stand for at least half an hour in
the vinegar, oil, and spices. You may also add slices of fresh
green chili pepper, or hot pepper if you like. Chill and serve.

BABI KECAP
Soy Sauce Pork

I first prepared Babi Kecap when I was thirteen, on the anniversary of the birthday of Princess Juliana of Holland, the daughter of Queen Wilhelmina. At the European school in Depok there were parties in all the classrooms. The girls wore orange ribbons and the boys wore orange pins in the form of daisies on their white shirts. We were served orange lemonade and biscuits with orange sugar sprinkled on top. Games were played and balloons were set loose in the air. Many Dutch songs could be heard from the classrooms.

But I remember that all the festivities were wasted on me that day because I was so anxious to get home and make my first real meat dish. I didn't even stay after school long enough to drink my lemonade, and when school was let out at noon that day, I ran all the way home, which was about five blocks from the school.

When I got home I ran straight to the kitchen, yelling, "Grandma, Grandma, did you get the meat yet?" I remember Grandma saying, "Calm down, calm down. Change your clothes first." I ran to my room and pulled off my school clothes and put on my play clothes which were coveralls with short pants.

Returning to the kitchen, I saw that there was a beautiful piece of pork loin on the table that had been neatly trimmed of the fat. Grandma gave me a sharp knife and had me cut the pork into small cubes, which I then put into a clay bowl before spicing.

I had watched Grandma make Babi Kecap many times, and I was so proud when it turned out just as it was supposed to. I was proud of my skill but even more proud because Grandma trusted me with such an expensive piece of meat. Of course I ruined many, many other dishes in the years ahead, but that Babi Kecap was almost perfect. My oldest brother gave me a great compliment, for him, when he said, "Not bad for a beginner." Poppie rewarded me with a twenty-five cent piece which I thought was a lot of money. I bought twenty-five big sourballs.

This is the recipe for Grandma's Babi Kecap:

BABI KECAP

Soy Sauce Pork
Serves 4 to 6

2 teaspoons salt
5 cloves fresh garlic *or* 2 teaspoons garlic granules
3 pounds pork loin, cut in one-inch cubes
2 teaspoons salt
5 cloves
5 cloves fresh garlic *or* 2 teaspoons garlic granules
1 three-inch piece fresh ginger
½ tablespoon ground black pepper
2 tablespoons oil
3 tablespoons brown sugar
½ onion, chopped
2 cups water
¼ cup kecap manis
juice of 1 lemon
chopped green onions

Grind the salt, cloves, garlic, ginger, and pepper in a mortar. Mix well with pieces of meat and let stand for at least ten minutes. Saute the meat and spices in the oil over a low fire with the brown sugar and chopped onions. Add the water and kecap manis and cover the pan, stirring occasionally so the meat doesn't stick to the pan. Simmer about half an hour until the water cooks away and the gravy is thick and dark. Then add lemon juice. The meat will be dark brown. Test with a fork to be sure it is tender, then serve hot with white rice. Top with green onions.

kecap manis
sweet soy sauce: p. 96

A Tempting Trio

SATE AYAM
Barbecued Chicken on Bamboo Skewers

I first cooked Sate Ayam after my fifth grade class made a field trip to the botanical gardens in Bogor, a city about fifteen miles from my hometown. Arriving on the bus with pencil and paper in hand, we were each to make a report on whatever plant or tree interested us. I wrote something about orchids.

The botanical gardens in Bogor were very beautiful, with huge trees, greenhouses, and plants from all over the world. On the same property was the palace of the Governor of Indonesia, surrounded by deep green lawns where tame peacocks, deer, and pheasant wandered all about.

From twelve-thirty to two we had a lunch break. I had been given two gulden to buy snacks and souvenirs from the vendors who lined the street outside the gardens. Some vendors sold rings made from nut shells and others sold jewelry pins made from brilliant colored coconut bugs. But my first steps took me straight to the food vendors and the many small eating stands. I was drawn to one in particular by the smell of cooking Sate Ayam. I saw small pieces of chicken marinating in two different kinds of sauces, one brown, the other yellow. I ordered six sticks of each and watched as the woman took the tiny pieces of meat from the marinade and placed them on bamboo sticks. While the meat was cooking, I asked the woman the ingredients of her marinades. She must have thought it funny that a girl as young as myself was asking such a question because she laughed. But, with a smile, she told me what the ingredients were, probably never thinking that I would remember them.

The next day I saw that one of the servants had killed a fat chicken, and I asked Grandma if I could try and make Sate Ayam. Of course I knew that Grandma would never refuse me. After I had cooked the Sate, I gave two pieces of each kind to Grandma for her verdict. Grandma told me that she preferred the Chinese-style sate, and also that I had slightly overcooked the chicken, but she said, "Don't feel badly about it, my dear. This is your first time and your spices were just perfect." To show me how proud she was, she took a nickel from the moneybag that was fastened around her waist by a gold chain. I hugged Grandma and kissed her on her cheek and she laughed and pushed me away, saying, "Come on, clean up before your father comes home and sees you so messy." I had smudges and ashes all over my hands, face, and clothes.

First, I will give you the recipe for Sate Madura, whose taste is supposed to have originated on the island of Madura, and then Sate Jakarta, whose taste is more Chinese. Here are the two Sates that I ate that day in Bogor.

SATE AYAM

Barbecued Chicken on Bamboo Skewers
Each recipe serves 2

Sate Ayam Madura

1 chicken breast, skinned, boned, and diced
2 teaspoons ground coriander
1½ teaspoons cumin
2 cloves fresh garlic, mashed or flattened with a cleaver
1 two-inch piece ginger, crushed
1 teaspoon black pepper
juice of ½ lemon
2 tablespoons brown sugar
1 teaspoon kunyit
½ teaspoon salt
1 tablespoon kecap manis

Mix all the spices with the chicken meat and let stand for at least 15 minutes, preferably longer. Place the meat on skewers and barbecue over a charcoal fire. Top with Bumbu Kacang, kecap manis, and bawang goreng, and serve with white rice and lemon slices.

kunyit
turmeric: p. 89

bawang goreng
fried onions: p. 91

kecap manis
sweet soy sauce: p. 96

Bumbu Kacang
peanut sauce: p. 33

Sate Ayam Jakarta

1 whole breast of chicken, skinned, boned, and diced *or*
  the equivalent of any kind of meat
2 cloves fresh garlic, crushed
1 tablespoon brown sugar
1 teaspoon ground white pepper
1 two-inch piece ginger, crushed
2 tablespoons kecap manis
1 tablespoon sesame oil
1 teaspoon sesame seeds
2 teaspoons green onions, chopped

Mix the chicken with the spices and allow to soak in. Place the meat on bamboo skewers and barbecue over a charcoal fire. Top with green onions, bawang goreng, and kecap manis, and serve with lemon slices.

UDANG GORENG
Fried Shrimp

Dear Grandchildren, this is a simple recipe, but it takes some practice. It is a recipe originally from Depok, although I have changed it a lot. Depok is about twenty-five miles from the ocean and shellfish were expensive—in those days, no one had refrigerators or freezers and saltwater fish had to be shipped in blocks of ice.

I remember that if we ate shrimp, Grandma was careful to count out an equal number for each of us children, usually six to eight shrimp each. My mouth waters, even today, if I think how good Grandma's shrimp tasted.

When I was eleven, I liked shrimp so much that I couldn't always wait until shrimp came from the coast. Just next to our house was a small creek that was always full of water. Many fish lived there as well as freshwater shrimp. One day I wanted shrimp so badly that I made a fishing pole from a bamboo stick, thread, and a bent needle from Mommie's sewing basket. I used the tinfoil from a cigarette package for a sinker, and I dug up small red worms from along the creek bank with my bare hands for bait. My fishing was very inefficient and it took me a long time to snag the shrimp. When I had about twelve shrimp, I ran home and prepared them as Grandma did, by marinating them in tamarind and salt, then frying them in coconut oil. I cleaned them by breaking off their heads and leaving the shell intact, Chinese style. I have several ways of cooking Udang Goreng—this is the recipe for fried shrimp that is so popular in my restaurant today.

UDANG GORENG

Fried Shrimp
Serves 1 or 2

2 teaspoons butter
juice of ½ clove fresh garlic
1 ounce *or* 2 tablespoons peeled asam with seeds
12 medium prawns (of the size 31-35 to the pound)
  or the equivalent
¼ cup lemon juice
¼ teaspoon salt
2 teaspoons green onions, chopped

Melt the butter along with garlic juice and peeled asam in a
small frying pan, but don't allow the butter to brown. Let
the butter, garlic, and asam soak until the butter cools
slightly. Peel and devein the shrimp, or leave in the shell if
you prefer. When you are ready to cook, put the frying pan
on a high fire and when the butter starts to froth, add the
shrimp. Sprinkle on the salt and fry the shrimp as quickly as
possible, turning them more rapidly as the pan becomes
hotter. As the shrimp turn pink, the asam will start to come
loose from its seeds and stick on the bottom of the pan.
While you turn the shrimp quickly, scrape the asam from
the pan bottom and it will adhere to the shrimp. When the

asam
tamarind: p. 86

79

shrimp are sufficiently pink and covered with fried asam, turn off the fire, and while shaking the pan, squeeze on the lemon juice. Remove immediately to a serving dish, top with chopped green onions, and serve with lemon slices.

The secret to this dish is to have a sufficiently hot frying pan, preferably stainless steel or aluminum, to which the asam will stick. Teflon doesn't work well here. The shrimp should just cover the bottom of the pan. The asam should be fresh and moist, but if they have become dried out, run hot water over them briefly to make them moist. Do not soak the asam, however, because they will never brown in the pan and the shrimp will emerge soggy.

The ingredients are quite simple, but the frying is tricky because it must be fast. It is worth the practice. You will see.

GADO GADO
Indonesian Salad

When I first came to America, I couldn't get over how easy it was to prepare food here compared to when I was in Depok. I still think about it each time I make Gado Gado. Depok was famous for its Gado Gado and there were little Gado Gado shacks almost every two blocks at the side of the road, usually in front of the proprietor's house. Gado Gado was the favorite snack of Depokers—in fact, a healthy and filling meal any time of the day.

When I was younger I sampled all the Gado Gado stands. But my favorite was run by an older husband and wife whose stand was alongside the railroad station. I studied their cooking very closely and my taste, though different, was closest to theirs. In spite of the fact that almost everyone used the same spices to prepare Gado Gado, each taste was unique. During the time when Japan occupied Indonesia, I had a Gado Gado shack where I prepared each order to the taste of the customer, and also served fried noodles.

Gado Gado is actually a vegetable salad served warm or cold with spiced peanut dressing. The preparation of Gado Gado begins, of course, with growing and preparing the peanuts. In those days, I was lucky because my father still owned two acres of peanut fields. After the peanuts were dried in the sun, they were placed in large bags, weighing almost one hundred pounds each, and half the bags were sold. The remaining quantity was the year's supply for our family.

To prepare the peanuts, I first had to remove them from the shells and then roast them. To roast peanuts, a large wok was filled with river sand and then heated over a wood fire. When the sand was hot, the peanuts were added and stirred constantly. They cooked evenly in about half an hour and turned golden brown. The peanuts and sand were then placed in a bamboo strainer big enough to let the sand pass through but not the peanuts. The sand was then placed back in the wok and the procedure was repeated over and over again. The roasted peanuts were then placed on a round, flat bamboo tray and rolled lightly with a wooden roller similar to a rolling pin, causing the skins to come loose. When the peanuts were tossed lightly in the wind, the skins blew free and the peanuts were ready to use.

In my little shack I had a steamer for the vegetables and a

large, almost flat stone mortar for grinding the spices. I always liked my Gado Gado with a lot of chili peppers, but I cooked for each individual's taste. First, I would put the desired amount of fresh chili peppers on the stone and grind them fine with the pestle. Then I would add the peanuts and grind them along with the salt, brown sugar, and shrimp paste. When the peanuts were smooth and creamy, I would slowly add hot water and finally the juice of half a lime. I then put the vegetables in a deep plate, poured the sauce over the top and mixed it well, finally topping with deep-fried shrimp chips. I worked from ten in the morning until ten at night, and at the end of the day, after preparing about seventy-five orders, my arm certainly ached. In fact, my arm and wrist were painful for several years, even after I no longer had my shack.

My Gado Gado shack was actually a converted small house, but most stands just had dirt floors with dogs, cats, and chickens running about. Of course there was no Health Department then that required perfect walls and floors. If there had been, Depok would probably never have been the home of so many good cooks.

GADO GADO

Indonesian Salad
Serves 2 to 4

5 cups cut mixed vegetables (carrots, green beans, white
    cabbage, etc.—use any of your favorite vegetables)
1 cup chunky peanut butter
2 teaspoons terasi
juice of 2 cloves fresh garlic, pressed
    or 1 teaspoon garlic granules
1 ½ teaspoons salt
2 tablespoons brown sugar
juice of 1 lemon *or* 2 tablespoons white vinegar
    or 2 tablespoons asam juice
2 teaspoons crushed dry chili peppers (optional)
2 cups boiling water

Mix all the ingredients, except the vegetables, thoroughly,
then add water slowly. (I have never found any electric
mixers that proved satisfactory for making Gado Gado, but
you may.) When the peanuts and spices are mixed and are
the consistency of a thick salad dressing, pour over your
favorite raw vegetables or those that have been boiled
lightly or steamed, then top with bawang goreng and
kerupuk. Of course there are other variations on Gado
Gado—the sauce may even be heated before it is served.
Also, by gently heating the sauce, it will become thicker.

    To make Gado Gado sauce more of a salad dressing than
part of a hearty meal, substitute vinegar for half the water.
Add 1 teaspoon ground kencur for an exotic, aromatic taste.

terasi	**asam**	**bawang goreng**
shrimp paste: p. 89	*tamarind: p. 86*	*fried onions: p. 91*
kerupuk	**kencur:** *p. 92*	
chips: p. 93		

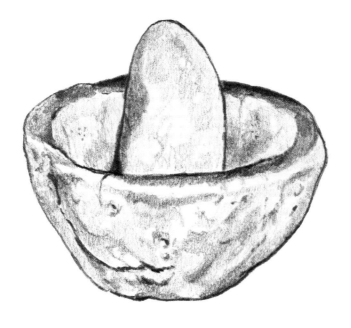

Spices

These are some of the spices and ingredients that give Indonesian food its unique taste. Because they are probably different than ingredients you are used to, I will tell you a little about them. There are many more spices that I will tell you about later, but these are the important ones, and the ones you will need for the recipes in this book.

If you are serious about being a good cook, you should have your own *cobek*, or stone mortar, and pestle for mashing and grinding spices. In Indonesia, such stones are greatly valued and treated as family heirlooms. It is my opinion that spices cannot be ground well in an electric mixer. Maybe I am just old-fashioned, or superstitious, but spices seem to lose their power and distinctness when sliced by metal blades, and the extent of mixing or grinding is too difficult to control.

The mortar I took to Holland and later brought to America has a bowl about the size of my two cupped hands, sufficient for almost all my needs. When I arrived in America, I also purchased a large flat stone in a Mexican grocery store for grinding large amounts of spices and grains. Before you use your stone the first time, soak it in water—and then treat it with respect. You may feel that it is part of you someday, and worthy of being passed on to your children or grandchildren.

ASAM
Tamarind

A huge tamarind tree grew in front of our house in Depok. The base of the tree was so big that ten men holding hands could not reach all the way around. According to Grandma, that tree was almost three hundred years old. As children, we used to enjoy eating its fruit dipped in crystallized sugar.

There are many tamarind trees in Indonesia and, I imagine, in most tropical countries. The leaves are dark green and delicate, similar to mimosa and acacia leaves. The fruit, which are produced after the tree is five years old, hang from the branches in large pods that look like giant beans, except that they are brown when mature. The shell of the pods are thin and hard, similar to lychee shells except smooth. Inside each pod are several hard, dark brown seeds in a row surrounded by meat which is soft, tangy, and sour.

In Mexico, I saw asam used for lemonade-like drinks as well as for candy and snacks. Indian people in Depok told me that in India it is used in many curry dishes and that goatherders carry tamarind water in goat bladders to combat the extreme heat.

In Indonesia, asam is an extremely important fruit—so important that the Indonesian word for sour is *asam*, and someone with a sour personality is an asam person. Asam is used for cooking all types of food dishes, as a drink, a snack, and medicine as well. I remember the first time I had my menstrual period, Grandma gave me a big glass of tamarind juice with a dash of kunyit, or turmeric powder, and two teaspoons of palm sugar. I had to drink a glass every morning before breakfast during my period. Grandma said that it was good for the blood and would keep a person young-looking and without wrinkles her entire life. I drank that concoction for many years.

In Indonesia, such tonics are called *jamu*, and similar recipes made from spices, fruit, roots, and flowers are popular with the entire population. Many recipes have been passed down from generation to generation for hundreds of years. Jamus are made, and sold, for every conceivable health purpose. The most famous and respected jamu company is Nyonya Meneer of Semerang, Middle Java. Grandma said that it is because of the spices, fruit, and especially chili peppers that Indonesian women keep good complexions.

Tamarind can be purchased fresh, in the shell, in many grocery stores that sell imported Mexican foods. For a while I even saw it sold in a large California supermarket chain store. It can also be purchased peeled and compressed or frozen in Dutch, Indian, Malaysian, Indonesian, and Philippine import stores. Some low-quality asam has been salted and some contains pieces of the shell. Such tamarind is usually sold for making juice.

Fresh tamarind keeps fairly well in the pod and can be peeled, compressed, and wrapped in cellophane or plastic wrap for storage. Asam can also be frozen but I think it loses much of its consistency and flavor when thawed.

In the recipes I have included in this book, the asam is to be peeled, but the seeds left intact. Some customers take the seeds home from my restaurant because they are extremely hard and appear polished. Many people use them to make jewelry or decorations.

Although tamarind juice is available bottled, as a beverage, for cooking it is too watery and does not have enough asam flavor. When asam juice is called for in a recipe, first peel fresh tamarind and place in a bowl, then pour over it enough hot water to cover. Squeeze the fruit by hand until the meat is sticky and comes away from the seeds. Strain through cheesecloth.

SEREH
Lemon Grass

I remember that when I was a young girl, Grandma rarely cut fresh sereh herself. She always waited until after I had taken my afternoon bath and then she would tell me exactly how many stalks she wanted me to cut. Grandma said that sereh would have a beautiful fragrance if it was cut by a virgin. (This was not because someone who was not a virgin was considered impure physically. It was that before her first sexual experience, a young woman's mind was clearer or more "pure.") How seriously Grandma took that Indonesian superstition I can't say, because she always wore her Buddha smile. But I know that Nanny and other Indonesian women, if there were no young girls present, would always wash, apply makeup, or straighten their hair before cutting sereh.

Although similar in appearance to regular grass, sereh grows in wide clumps and up to two feet tall and higher. The leaves are not actually single, but grow from stalks that separate into single-appearing grasslike blades that are long and green, have sharp edges, and droop over when mature.

Sereh can be bought in many stores, especially in Chinese, Southeast Asian, and Mexican import stores. It is the base of the sereh stalk, to about four or five inches, that contains the best flavor, so the best quality sereh is usually sold in thick, whole pieces. In packages that contain cut pieces of lemon grass, look for curved pieces that are cut from the layered base of the stalk, not flat pieces that are cut from the single top of a blade or leaf.

Don't expect the very subtle taste of sereh to dominate the flavoring of a dish. It is used extensively in Indonesian cooking because of the tangy aromatic taste that it imparts to a dish. Of course there are recipes that make sereh the dominant taste, but I will tell you of those later.

Sereh is tough and should not be eaten by itself. When used in Indonesian cooking, pieces of the base of the lemon grass are usually left whole or sliced lengthwise to allow more of the flavor to escape. These may be removed from the dish just before serving. When used for making tea, it may be chopped.

Sereh grows in many tropical countries. I grow sereh for my restaurant in a greenhouse because it must be kept from freezing. In southern California, a friend grows sereh outdoors all year around. It likes a lot of sun and water. The plant multiplies rapidly and when it is trimmed by removing stalks at the base, it seems to grow even faster.

Because it is so easily stored and packaged, sereh is used extensively for the lemon flavor it imparts to many edible products. It is also used for tea, in cosmetics, and as a medicine throughout the world.

JAHE
Ginger

Ginger is similar to the cana plant that grows in America, with large, firm leaves that grow on both sides of a watery stem. The flowers are a beautiful white, and similar to an orchid.

Ginger root is used in many Chinese dishes and in India it is used in curry dishes. Ginger is also used as a medicine for colds and coughs. I have never bothered to grow ginger root in my greenhouse in America because it is so available here. In

Indonesia, ginger is also the base for a drink that is sold at roadside stands as a hot punch called *bandrek*. You make bandrek by boiling palm sugar, cloves, cinnamon sticks, and ginger in water. It is served hot with many kinds of snacks.

KUNYIT
Turmeric

Kunyit, or turmeric, is a member of the ginger family, but the leaves are smaller and light green. The root is also smaller than ginger and is a light golden yellow. It is used for cooking and for medicine. Grandma said that we shouldn't use the main part of the root for spice, but instead use the small side roots that branch off, because the taste is more flavorful and not so strong. Turmeric is grown in India, Indonesia, and many tropical countries. The leaves are similar to the leaves of the cana plant but more delicate. In Indonesia, the leaves are used for wrapping fish or meat and when barbecued, they give a delicious fragrance to the food. In India, kunyit is very popular because the dry, ground powder is the base for almost all curries.

Fresh kunyit is more delicious than powdered, but as it usually can't be bought here, ground turmeric is acceptable. When buying ground turmeric, remember that dark orange powder is from the main part of the root. It is the lowest quality, and may be bitter. Light golden-yellow powder is of the best quality and comes from the small side roots. Of course, most spice companies just grind the whole root together because the quality of turmeric is not common knowledge in most parts of the world.

I grow kunyit in small quantities in my greenhouse, and it doesn't take a lot of care. I especially like a mild crab curry made with sliced, fresh kunyit root. Someday I will make it for you.

TERASI
Shrimp or Prawn Paste

Terasi, or shrimp paste, is made from shrimp that have been boiled, then ground to a paste, mixed with salt and rice flour, and then formed into small bricks that are often dried in the sun. Many people unfamiliar with terasi use the paste without realizing that it must be roasted first before being used for cooking, so that the overly strong taste and smell are removed. In the Philippines, shrimp paste is made with a liquid base. In

Indonesia, there are three qualities of terasi. The lowest, third quality, terasi is made from the head, shell, and tails of the shrimp as well as parts of other fish. Second quality is made from whole shrimp, but no other fish. First quality is made from only the main body of the peeled shrimp.

Grandma would only buy the best terasi from vendors she knew personally. Her favorite brands were imported from Hong Kong and Jirebon in East Java. Grandma always roasted the terasi on a solid heavy grill, then stored it in an airtight container. Just before using it, she ground it in a mortar and then added it to the food.

To prepare block terasi, it should be cut into ¼" slices and then placed on tinfoil or a pan in a 300° oven until it dries out and browns with a light crust. If your oven is vented, your neighbors will probably go indoors. If it is not, you will probably go outdoors. The smell of terasi is infamous and I won't describe it here. But the spice you will have is worth the temporary bad odor.

DAUN SALAM
Indonesian Salam Leaf

The salam tree produces one of the most used spices in Indonesia, but as popular as it is, I have never heard of anyone ever planting a salam tree. They grow wild everywhere. And because almost everyone pinches the leaves, most trees have a bushy appearance. When the trees are in fruit, dark red berries similar in appearance to cherries hang from the branches. The round seed inside the berry is similar to a cherry pit. When we were children, we used to pick the berries up from the ground and eat them.

When the trees were in fruit, hundreds of different kinds of birds gathered in the branches. Because of the berries, the trees were also one of the favorite places of what we called *kalong*, or flying dogs. These were actually fox bats—giant bats with faces like foxes and a wingspan of three or four feet. In the daytime, their huge forms could be seen hanging in the topmost branches.

I would not suggest substituting any other leaf for daun salam. It would be better to leave it out altogether. A good dish will still be good.

BAWANG GORENG
Fried Onions

Bawang goreng are thinly sliced, deep-fried onions. In Indonesia, we had only small onions with paper-thin skins which were tastier than large onions but more difficult to prepare. Of course, imported California onions were also available, but they were too expensive to use, as bawang goreng was served with so many dishes—most often as a topping and with sayurs. I have found that firm white onions make the best bawang goreng, but any firm onions are satisfactory.

It is important to slice the onions very evenly so that they will brown identically. Using an electric slicer is the easiest way to do this. First, slice the onion in half, lengthwise, through the ends, and remove the outer skin. Then cut thin slices from one end to the other—not so thin that the slices lose their form but just thick enough so that they retain their individual shape when piled up. The slices can be mixed by hand so that each piece is separated and can be cooked from all sides. Salt is often squeezed by hand into the onion slices to make them crisper.

Heat an amount of oil, equal in volume to the sliced onions, to a temperature that causes one small piece of onion to rise immediately to the top of the oil, but not so hot that it then runs around the top of the oil. Place the onions in the oil, taking care that the oil doesn't bubble over the edge of the pan. Stir immediately to further separate the onion pieces, then stir occasionally every few minutes. The fire should be as high as possible—the bubbling will subside as the onions cook. When the onions are almost done, and have lost most of their water, they will need constant stirring as they brown. When done, the onions will rise up noticeably to the top of the oil. Continue stirring until all the onions are a golden brown. Drain, then place on paper towels. When the onion pieces have cooled enough to become crispy, place in an airtight container. Do not allow the onions to remain on the towels until they become completely cold, as the oil will soak back into the onions, making them soggy.

Because of the time involved in cooking (up to one hour for twelve large onions), it is best to cook as many onions as possible and then store for future use. A frying basket that can be lifted from the oil when the onions are done makes the job much easier.

TEMU KUNCI

Because the roots are so watery, temu kunci is very difficult to keep fresh, and as far as I know, is available fresh only in Indonesia. In powdered form, it is available in Dutch and Indonesian import stores.

Temu kunci roots are similar in appearance to the air roots that grow on the houseplants known in America as spiderplants—small, thin, translucent, almost like baby fingers. The fragrance of the root is indescribable. I don't remember temu kunci being used in more than a few dishes—in East Java, it is used in salads, and for medicinal purposes.

KEMIRI
Candlenuts

Kemiri nuts are used in Indonesian cooking to give many dishes a nutty flavor. Kemiri nuts grow on large trees that have large round leaves. There is a fine golden-brown powder on the underside of the leaves, and if the sun is shining and the wind blowing, it looks as if all the leaves are sprinkled with gold dust. The kemiri nuts are actually the seeds of the kemiri fruit that look like green balls hanging down from the branches. Sometimes they grow almost as large as soccer balls. When the fruit is ripe, it splits open and all the kemiri nuts fall out onto the ground. The small kemiri nuts, the size of marbles, have thick, dark grey shells, almost as thick as coconut shells. They look like rocks and are almost as hard. Inside is the kernel which is used in cooking and for making oil. The oil is especially good for the hair and scalp.

If you cannot find kemiri, macadamia nuts may be substituted.

KENCUR

Kencur is a dark brown root that has the appearance of little balls, almost like marbles. The small curly leaves of the plant are similar to turmeric leaves, but they grow right on the ground, without stems. The plants are so tender that I have never been able to transfer them to my greenhouse. It is my feeling that the taste of the kencur root, except in the smallest amounts, is too strong for most Americans and Europeans who are not accustomed to strange tastes.

Kencur roots are sold in most Chinese groceries and drugstores to be mixed with other herbs for cough medicine and other ailments. In Indonesia, it is also used as a medicine. By grinding the root with rice flour and mixing with vinegar, a paste is made which is applied to sprained ankles and painful muscles. I have used it many times that way and found it to be warm on the skin, almost like menthol.

KERUPUK

Kerupuk is roughly translated as chip, as in potato chip. Kerupuk are made from rice flour, flavoring, and sometimes coloring. Kerupuk udang are made from shrimp and kerupuk ikan from fish. After a dough has been made and has dried to very hard, cracker-like pieces, the chips are deep-fried in oil where they puff up to double or triple their original size. Kerupuk should be stored in an airtight container and not fried until they are to be eaten. If the kerupuk become damp, they should be dried in the sun or in an oven prior to frying. There are many different kinds and shapes of kerupuk, and in villages they can be seen drying in bamboo trays on rooftops. Many kinds of kerupuk are named for the particular region where they originated or where they were produced.

The best kerupuk can be purchased in Indonesian and Malaysian import stores. They have a rich, distinct taste and texture. Unfortunately, they are quite expensive to buy in large quantities. For that reason, in my restaurant I substitute a Chinese variety of kerupuk that can be bought in most Chinese groceries. Although the shrimp taste is often hardly discernible, they are called "shrimp chips." If you want to buy real kerupuk, the two most available are kerupuk udang Palembang and kerupuk Sidoardjo.

LAOS
Red Ginger

Laos grows in the same manner as ginger. The only difference between the plants is that while ginger has dark green leaves and white flowers, laos has dark green, red-veined leaves and red flowers. Laos is used for both cooking and medicine. I remember that Grandma used young laos root in a famous sauce for barbecued fish, and in a few other dishes. I don't use laos in too many dishes that I cook for Europeans and Americans because the taste is quite strong.

GULA JAWA
Java Palm Sugar

Gula jawa is a dark brown sugar made from the aren palm tree. It is usually sold in block or cylindrical form. Palm sugar can be bought in many Indonesian and Malaysian import stores, and can also be found in Mexican groceries. Because gula jawa is not that available, for these recipes I have substituted dark brown sugar that can be bought in any supermarket. If you can find gula jawa, just use the same amount of it as brown sugar called for in the recipes.

SANTAN
Coconut Juice

The term "coconut juice" is often misunderstood. Many think that coconut juice is the thin liquid that is inside a coconut. I call that coconut milk. Coconut milk is very refreshing, but I remember that as a young girl I was told it was not good for a young woman or girl to drink it because it would cause the female organs to be too moist. Coconut milk was considered bad for athletes because it caused a weakness of the knees. How true this is, I was never able to find out.

In Indonesia we have at least five different kinds of coconut. *Kelapa ijo*, or green coconut, has a green shell with pink on the top and never changes color as it matures, as does the regular coconut. This variety is used for medicinal purposes or special offerings to the spirits. Then there is another kind called *kelapa puyu*, or dwarf coconut. This tree doesn't grow any larger than five or six feet and produces a coconut as small as a softball.

The coconut tree is very useful. The dry leaves are used for shade coverings and fresh leaves are used for decorations at parties and weddings. The hairy covering of the coconut husk is used for rope, brooms, brushes, and as a wrapping when layering plants in the garden. It is also used to grow orchids on.

Santan, or coconut juice, is best when made from fresh, peeled coconut meat. Place one-inch square pieces in a blender with an equal amount of water and blend for several minutes. Pour into a strainer or into cheesecloth, pressing the juice through with the fingers. Then squeeze any remaining juice out of the pulp by hand. If no blender is available, the coconut meat may be grated into a bowl, adding an equal amount of water, and then squeezing with the hands at least twenty times and straining as above. To make santan with dried coconut, soak it in hot water for at least five minutes and then blend as above and strain. One cup of coconut and one cup of water will produce about a cup of coconut juice. The less water used, the richer the santan will be. Coconut juice does not keep well unless it is frozen, so make just what you will use immediately or make enough to freeze for future use.

Coconut juice is now available frozen in many import stores as well as in supermarket gourmet sections. Coconut juice can also be bought in cans, although this is often the most expensive method and often sugar has been added. Avoid buying coconut creme, however, which is the top of the coconut juice after it has been allowed to stand. In Indonesia, cooking is usually done with coconut juice and not with creme.

KECAP MANIS
Indonesian Sweet Soy Sauce

When I was in Indonesia, I never learned how to make soy sauce from scratch, because it could be bought everywhere and Grandma said it was hard to make. Indonesians cook with a sweet soy sauce, whereas Chinese cook with a salty soy sauce and then add almost no salt to their food. In Indonesia, there were three kinds of Chinese soy sauce: shrimp flavored, fish flavored, and regular soy sauce which tasted like ordinary soy sauce that can be bought here in America.

When I first went to Holland in 1945, I was desperate because there was no sweet soy sauce to be found, only the salty Chinese kind. I devised a recipe for making sweet soy sauce from salty soy sauce, and I still prepare kecap manis the same way in my restaurant now.

KECAP MANIS

Indonesian Sweet Soy Sauce

1¼ cups of Kikkoman-style soy sauce
2¼ cups dark brown sugar
1 cup corn syrup
¾ cup water
2½ tablespoons flour
4 dry shrimp

Mix the flour with a small portion of the water, and when smooth, add to the other ingredients in a large pan. Mix well and place on a high fire. Stir occasionally until the mixture boils. It is hard to notice that the sauce is boiling as the bubbles are quite small. You will see, however, that the level of the liquid in the pan rises noticeably. Pay close attention to the level of the liquid as it starts to boil, because if left unattended, the kecap manis will very quickly boil up and over the edge of the pan and create a sticky, messy spill. Remove from the fire and cool. Strain through cheesecloth and bottle for storage.

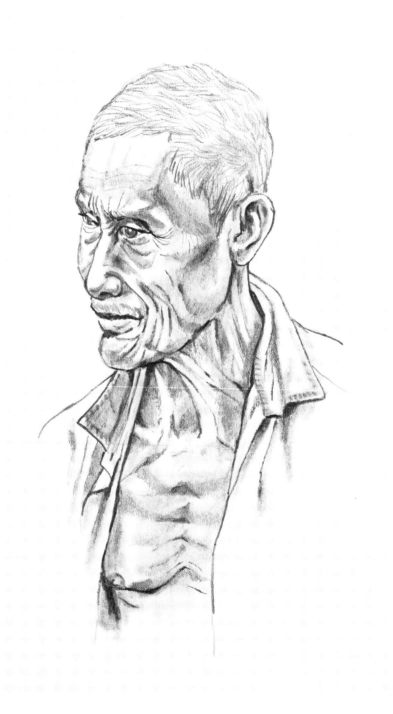

Afterword

You, my grandchildren, have the blood of many races and so are greatly blessed. I remember that it was shortly after my sixteenth birthday when I was told that I would have to marry, and I was so unhappy. But my Grandpa Samuel told me not to feel badly. He said that because I was marrying a European, my children would be of mixed blood and would acquire the best traits of each race. He thought that Depok "blood" was getting old and weak. He said that my children would bring me happiness, and it is true because they gave me all of you.

If you inherit anything from my family, I hope that you will love to cook. To be a good cook, you must learn, as I did from Grandma, to enjoy different tastes and to love cooking for other people's tastes as much as for your own. My wish, too, is that you will have a respect for Nature and that you will be superstitious—superstitious enough to believe in everything good that your mind can imagine.

I hope that all of you, my dear grandchildren, have enjoyed these cooking lessons. My Grandma and my Nanny, who were my first teachers, always made cooking an important game, and I enjoyed every minute of it. I hope you will enjoy it, too. If there is time, maybe I can teach you through tasting. But I will write more for you because I had many other teachers, and there is so much more to tell.

I would like to thank my husband Bill, Sarah, Christopher, and Alonso for their encouragement and help in making this gift possible.

Glossary

acar (*ah* char), pickled

asam (*ah* sm), tamarind; sour

ayam (*ah* yahm), chicken

babi (*bah* bee), pig

bakar (*bah* kahr), baked; to bake; burn

bapak (*bah* pah), father; respectful way of addressing older man

bandrek (*bahn* drek), hot punch, made by boiling palm sugar, cloves, cinnamon sticks, and ginger in water

bawang (*bah* wahng), onion

bawang goreng (*bah* wahng *gohr* eng), fried onions

bayem (*bye* ehm), spinach

besar (beh *sahr*), big

betel nut = pinang (*pee* nahng), a small hard palm-nut that is scraped, wrapped in a fresh ciri leaf with powdered lime and sometimes other spices, and chewed like tobacco as a stimulant

brandal (*brahn* dahl), bratty; disobedient

bumbu (*boom* boo), spices; ingredients

buncis (*boon* chees), green beans

ca (*cha*), sauteed

cabe (*cha* bay), chili pepper

campur (*chahm* poor), mixed; to mix

cobek (cho *bek*), also **chowet** (chow *eht*), stone mortar used to grind spices

Cirebon (chee *ray* bohn), a city in East Java

ciri (*see* ree), leaf used to wrap betel nut scrapings to be chewed

daging (*dah* geeng), meat; **daging babi**, pork meat

daun (*dah* oon), leaf

daun salam (*dah* oon sah *lahm*), salam leaf which is a widely-used spice in Indonesian cuisine

Dewi Sri (*day* wee *sree*), Javanese Goddess of Rice

duku (*doo* koo), a tree and its fruit which is marble-sized with a brittle shell encasing a delicately flavored grape-like kernel

dukun (*doo* koon), a person with paranormal mental abilities

gado gado (*gah* doh *gah* doh), Indonesian vegetable dish

garam (*gah* rahm), salt

goreng (*gohr* eng), fried

grobak (*gro* bek), two-wheeled open wooden cart

gula (*goo* lah), sugar

gula jawa (*goo* lah *jah* wah), "Java sugar," or brown sugar from the aren palm tree

ibu (*ee* boo), mother

ijo (*ee* joh), green

ikan (*ee* kahn), fish

jahe (*jah* hay), ginger

jamu (*jah* moo), herbal medicine

Java (*jah* wah), Java

kacang (kah *chang*), peanut(s)

kalong (*kah* long), fox bats

kambing (*kahm* bing), goat

kampong (*kahm* pong), jungle village(s)

karbau (kar *bow*), a type of water buffalo

kebaya (keh *bye* ah), blouse

kecap (*keh* chop), soy sauce

kecap manis (*keh* chop *mah* nees), Indonesian sweet soy sauce

kelapa (*klah* pah), coconut

kemiri (keh *meh* ree), candlenut

kerbau (kahr *bow*), a type of water buffalo

kerupuk (*kroo* pook), deep-fried, flavored chips

ketimun (keh *tee* moon), cucumber

kunyit (koon *yeet*), turmeric

laos (*lah* ohs), red ginger

luwak (*loo* wahk), small, furry, squirrel-like animals

mandur (mahn *doohr*), foreman

manis (*mah* nees), sweet

muda (*moo* dah), young

nasi (*nah* see), rice

nasi goreng (*nah* see *gohr* eng), fried rice

nasi uduk (*nah* see *oo* dook), rice cooked in coconut juice

Nyonya (*nyoh* nhah), Mistress; Mrs.

oom (*ohm*), uncle; a respectful way of addressing a man

oma (*oh* mah), grandmother; a respectful way of addressing a woman old enough to be a grandmother

pandan wangi (*pahn* dahn *wahng* ee), a bush whose leaves are used for flavoring and coloring

panggang (*pahng* gahng), barbecued

pepes (peh *pehs*), cooked by wrapping in a leaf

perkedel bakar (*per* kah del *bah* kar), Indonesian meat loaf

perkedel goreng (*per* kah del *goh* reng), deep-fried meat balls

pohon (poh *hohn*), tree

pohon kelapa (poh *hohn klah* pah), coconut tree

puyu (*poo* yoo), small; miniature

rijsttaffel (*rice* tah fuhl) [Dutch], huge meals prepared by the Dutch colonists that were comprised of many different Indonesian dishes and required numerous cooks and waiters to serve, always with rice as the central dish; also, a term used in Holland for an Indonesian meal

sambal (*sahm* bahl), condiment; hot sauce

sapi (*sah* pee), beef

santan (*sahn* tahn), coconut juice derived from coconut meat blended with water, then strained

sate (*sah* tay), meat, fowl, or fish barbecued on bamboo skewers

sawah (*sah* wah), wet rice fields

sayur (*sah* yoor), Indonesian vegetable dish served in a watery broth which in some dishes is soup-like

sedap (seh *duhp*), tasty; delicious

sereh (seh *reh*), lemon grass

tahu (*tah* hoo), beancake; tofu

tangan (*tahn* gahn), hand

tekie (*teh* kee), small edible roots

telur (tel *uhr*), egg(s)

temu kunci (*teh* moo *koon* chee), Indonesian root used as a spice

terasi (*trah* see), shrimp paste

tumis (*too* mees), sauteed

udang (*oo* dahng), shrimp

NOTES

NOTES